William Colson Westlake

**The Sure Foundation**

Or Past and Future of the Society of Friends

William Colson Westlake

**The Sure Foundation**
*Or Past and Future of the Society of Friends*

ISBN/EAN: 9783337073954

Printed in Europe, USA, Canada, Australia, Japan

Cover: Foto ©ninafisch / pixelio.de

More available books at **www.hansebooks.com**

# THE SURE FOUNDATION;

OR,

## PAST AND FUTURE

OF THE

## SOCIETY OF FRIENDS.

WITH

A SUPPLEMENTAL CHAPTER

ON SOME OF THE ESSAYS ALREADY PUBLISHED.

BY

W. C. WESTLAKE.

". . . . BUILT UPON THE FOUNDATION OF THE APOSTLES AND PROPHETS, JESUS CHRIST HIMSELF BEING THE CHIEF CORNER-STONE."—EPH. II. 20.

LONDON:
A. W. BENNETT, 5, BISHOPSGATE STREET WITHOUT.
DUBLIN: HODGES AND SMITH.

MDCCCLX.

*Price 2s. 6d.*

# PREFACE.

The annexed advertisement, which appeared in the public prints, will explain the origin of this essay:—

### SOCIETY OF FRIENDS.

#### PRIZE ESSAY.

A Gentleman who laments that notwithstanding the population of the United Kingdom has more than doubled itself in the last fifty years, the Society of Friends is less in number than at the beginning of the century; and who believes that the Society at one time bore a powerful witness to the world concerning some of the errors to which it is most prone, and some of the truths which are the most necessary to it; and that this witness has been gradually becoming more and more feeble, is anxious to obtain light respecting the causes of this change. He offers a PRIZE of ONE HUNDRED GUINEAS for the best ESSAY that shall be written on the subject, and a PRIZE of FIFTY GUINEAS for the one next in merit. He has asked three gentlemen, not members of the Society of Friends, to pronounce judgment on the Essays which shall be sent to them. They have all some acquaintance with the history of the Society, and some interest in its existing members; and as they are likely to regard the subject from different points of view, he trusts that their decision will be impartial; that they will not expect to find their own opinions represented in the Essays; and that they will choose the one which exhibits most thought and Christian earnestness, whether it is favourable or unfavourable to the Society, whether it refers the diminution of its influence to degeneracy, to something wrong in the original constitution of the body, to the rules which it has adopted for its government, or to any extraneous cause.

Rev. F. D. MAURICE, Chaplain of Lincoln's Inn; Professor J. P. NICHOLL, Glasgow; and Rev. E. S. PRYCE, Gravesend, have agreed to act as Adjudicators.

This invitation was responded to by about one hundred

and fifty writers, and a few months since the two prizes were awarded.

It is an unusual circumstance for an admirer of any sect to offer a public prize for discovering its failings without reference to its excellencies; and still more so, to select as judges three eminent writers, none of whom agree with its fundamental views. If the soundness of the main doctrines of Friends had been the required postulate upon which all essays should be based, the result would have been less singular. By the present mode, not only has full scope been given to those who (like the author of the second prize essay) condemn every thing which is opposed to Anglo-catholicism; but, on the other hand, those who would uphold Quakerism, have, from the nature of the advertisement, been discouraged from making allusion to its merits, and been specially occupied in setting forth its faults.

The impulse, thus unintentionally given by the prize donor, to write down the principle as well as the practices of this Society, has brought to light eight or ten printed essays, all of which are of necessity more or less fault-finding, and one or two directly antagonistic. Such an one-sided contemplation of its tenets by one hundred and fifty essayists would be an extremely severe ordeal for any sect, but it is especially so for the Friends, whose practices differ in many respects from other Christian communities. No fair exposition can be arrived at by looking only upon the dark side; and the present essay is published at the request of several friends, who think it embraces a fuller and more just view of Quakerism.

Notwithstanding that the Society of Friends has thus been placed very disadvantageously before the religious world of 1860, the writer is far from regretting the circumstances which have occasioned it. A Christian church which had settled down too much at its ease concerning the souls of perishing multitudes around it, and which was hiding its light within its own narrow borders, ought to profit from such an united assault from friends and foes. If, instead of despising these strictures, it proceeds in deep humility and contrition to examine them, we shall find that, as of old, "out of the eater shall come forth meat, and out of the strong shall come forth sweetness." If turned to proper account, such trials are blessed of God to the purifying of the church; but if unheeded, they increase its condemnation, and hasten it onwards to a condition yet lower and more lifeless.

Whilst endeavouring to reach the real causes of decline, the writer found that there was involved a still more important question, viz., *the causes of vitality.* The investigation into which he has thus been led, has resulted in strengthening his convictions that the foundations of Quakerism stand sure. It has shewn him the excellence of many testimonies now half obscured by formalism and tradition, and proved how entirely the doctrines of Friends are in accordance with the deductions of reason, and with the truths of Holy Scripture. It has also clearly convinced him that ordinary pursuits and worldly avocations are not only compatible with a daily life of faith, but with the exercise of every spiritual gift in the church.

If, by the divine blessing on so slender a means, the perusal of the following pages should confirm any of his brethren in the same faith, the main object of publication will have been answered.

The essay having been composed during the active engagements of a mercantile life, renders the style somewhat detached and unequal, but it seeks no claim on the ground of literary merit. Since its return from the adjudicators it has been revised and somewhat shortened, and a few fresh notes have been added.

There will probably be found within its pages much that will be sympathized with by one class of his fellow-professors, and suggestions that will be painful to others; it must also contain sentiments differing from those held by his friends of other religious persuasions. Sensible of his own imperfections, the author, whilst expressing his convictions clearly and unhesitatingly, has endeavoured to do it with that charity which should interflow not only between individuals of the same sect, but between all members of the Church universal.

In now placing this volume before the public, it is with the heartfelt prayer, that whatever it contains of truth may be blessed of God the Holy Spirit unto the comfort and edification of the reader, and that its human errors may, by the same restraining grace, be prevented from offending the least of His little ones.

SOUTHAMPTON,
    *4th Mo. 5th*, 1860.

# CONTENTS.

|  | PAGE |
|---|---|
| **CHAPTER I.** | |
| Origin of the Society of Friends | 1 |
| **CHAPTER II.** | |
| Fundamental Doctrines | 11 |
| **CHAPTER III.** | |
| Testimonies | 29 |
| **CHAPTER IV.** | |
| Statistics | 37 |
| **CHAPTER V.** | |
| Progressive Development | 43 |
| **CHAPTER VI.** | |
| Impediments—Essential | 51 |
| **CHAPTER VII.** | |
| Impediments—Superficial: | |
| Part 1.—Misimpressions | 55 |
| Part 2.—Language and Dress | 65 |
| Part 3.—Deficiencies | 75 |
| Part 4.—Over-legislation | 78 |
| **CHAPTER VIII.** | |
| Concluding Remarks | 84 |
| **SUPPLEMENTAL CHAPTER** | 100 |

## TO THE ADJUDICATORS.

In the following essay the writer has felt that, in order to ascertain the causes of weakness in any structure (either material or spiritual), it is needful to test every part of the building, and to probe the sound as well as the unsound.

From the wording of the Advertisement he has also considered that the intention of the donor is not simply to procure a dry analysis or logical exposition of the supposed "feebleness," but that restorative suggestions are in accordance with the object desired.

CANDIDE ET CONSTANTER.

# PRESENT AND FUTURE

OF THE

# SOCIETY OF FRIENDS.

## CHAPTER I.

### ORIGIN.

In considering the past and present state of the religious Society of Friends, a short account of its origin and of its tenets and practices is needful, to enable the general reader to understand the nature of those hindrances which have operated against the spread of its religious principles.

The period at which it arose (in 1650) was one of great political and religious excitement. The Reformation of the sixteenth century had, by throwing aside the accumulated and darkening corruptions of popery, done much towards restoring Christianity to its original purity; and had established in this kingdom those two great bulwarks of religious freedom—viz., the right of private judgment, and the printing of the Holy Scriptures in the vulgar tongue. But although much was accomplished, much was left among the protestant reformed churches, which had no authority from scripture, nor justification on the ground of a needful expediency.*

* The changes effected by Luther and his cotemporaries were so vast and important, that, dazzled by their splendour, we are tempted to consider them as a complete instead of a partial work, and to overlook the

B

In this country, the founders of the English established church were men of great zeal, piety, and wisdom—men who nobly offered up their lives, as well as their possessions, for the cause of Christ, and for the spreading of His kingdom on earth. But it was not to be expected that they could accomplish everything that was needful, or that they would perceive and sweep away all the gross accumulations which had for centuries bedimmed the Christian faith; to the puritans and other nonconformist divines was left the task of further purification. These again retained amongst them views and practices not in accordance with the spirituality of the gospel dispensation.

The same blessed Spirit which called forth these various servants of the Lord to labour in His vineyard, was the origin and producer (as the first Friends believed) of a yet further reformation in the Christian church—a reformation in its practices, as well as in its faith. The dissolute lives of many high professors in that day, and their neglect of the flock over which they were appointed,* was in marked contrast to the external strictness of the puritans; but the great political and ecclesiastical changes in this country produced very little permanent

many phases in which they fell short of apostolic simplicity. By regarding either this epoch or that of the early Fathers as the fountain-heads of truth, we merely quench our thirst at impoverished human cisterns, instead of going back to that primeval source from which they drank, and from whence alone their strength was gathered. Have we not the same inspired volume to consult, and the same Holy Spirit to enlighten us?

* Much has lately been written upon the violent language and conduct of Fox and his brethren. In mitigation of this fault we must, however, bear in mind, not only the violent character of the age itself, and the thundering with which Huss, Luther, Knox, and other great reformers, assailed their opponents; but also the frightful state of irreligion and immorality in which Lord Macaulay depicts the clergy of that day (*History of England*, vol. i.).

religious benefit to the people at large, whose lives were passed either in the neglect of everything sacred, or else in an over-estimate and pharisaic observance of the external forms of religion.

It was at this period that George Fox, a young man of earnest life and strong convictions, after long preparation and a patient endurance of deep mental conflicts —after close and prayerful searching of the Scriptures and of his own heart, went forth to re-proclaim the spirituality of the gospel dispensation, and to bring about a revival of primitive Christianity and vital godliness. A remarkable power attended his preaching, and through his instrumentality very many others of all ranks were raised up to declare, in a similar way, the "unsearchable riches of Christ." Quakerism is therefore not to be regarded as a revelation of any new truth, or as any addition to primitive Christianity. It was stated by its founders to be that same Truth which was declared from the beginning, but which the traditions and maxims of men had, during the dark ages, overlaid and obscured.

It must ever be borne in mind that whilst all the works of God, both natural and spiritual, have a constant progressive tendency towards perfection — "first the blade, then the ear, then the full corn in the ear"— those of fallen man are constantly retrograde. However clear the fountain, or pure the resolve, it is found with churches, as with individuals, that impurity and apathy creep in by steps gradual but sure, and (unless prevented by divine grace) the machinery and adaptation of man will multiply errors and imperfections. History would also seem to prove it to be in accordance with the divine economy, that these subtractions and additions of man should from age to age be counteracted by a re-formation or a returning to first principles. Whilst the church of Christ ever remains the same, every branch of it finds itself, as years roll on, to be retrograde and not progressive; *e.g.*, the English protestants abandoned the errors of popery, and two centuries afterwards the Wesleyans, as holding a purer and more zealous faith, emerged from the English church; then again we have the reformed Methodists from out of these.

It is not my object here to discuss the extent or soundness of these secessions, but to point to the fact that nearly every instance of religious revival in any church ends in the secession of many of its most attached members, and in the establishment of some new sect professing a nearer approach to apostolic practice than that from which they seceded.

We find that the same truths implanted in the minds of the stern Roman, the wise Greek, or the strict Jew, brought forth different (but not opposite) external fruits. The admittance of the Gentiles into the fulness of the Gospel blessing, which needed a vision from heaven before the mind of Peter or James could be convinced thereof, was by Paul comprehended without effort. Notwithstanding the frequent declaration of our Saviour, that the old law was fulfilled or closed in Him, the disciples clung to the necessity of outward rites as accompanying salvation. Even eighteen years after the outpouring of the Holy Spirit on the day of Pentecost, when the whole church met at Jerusalem (Acts xv.), it was maintained by many of the believers, both in relation to Jewish and Gentile converts, "Except ye be circumcised after the manner of Moses ye cannot be saved." So strongly was this doctrine upheld, that, to subvert it, Peter had to refer to his divine mission to the Gentiles ten years before, and to the fact of these having received the Holy Ghost without circumcision, "their hearts having been purified by faith." This statement was followed by a narration from Paul and Barnabas of the wonders God had wrought amongst the Gentiles through them; and the proceedings were summed up by the Apostle James, who proposed that Gentile converts should not be interfered with; because, said he, "in every city Moses hath them that preach him, being read in their synagogues every Sabbath-day." Their views were so diverse, that but for this conference, it is probable that separate churches of Peter, James, or Paul, would have been then founded, and sectarianism thus early commenced. It is, however, remarkable that whilst they refrained from offering to Jewish believers any counsel upon the *impropriety* of longer keeping the Mosaic law, they unitedly insisted that all converts, whether Jew or Gentile, must "observe these necessary things"—viz., "abstaining from meats offered to idols, and from blood, and from things strangled, and from fornication;" thus upholding the Jewish law respecting things strangled, and placing it upon a par with the sin of fornication.* Again, A.D. 66, James and the elders, speaking to Paul of the many thousands of Jews which believe, state "They are all zealous of the law, and are informed of thee that thou teachest all the Jews which are amongst the Gentiles to forsake Moses," &c.; and instead of encouraging

---

* It is worthy of special note that, although the actions of Peter and James were so strongly tinctured with Judaism, yet their written epistles are not so. Even the epistle of James, which is full of minute instructions to believers, contains no allusion to outward ordinances of any kind. As inspired writers of Scripture, they were the mouthpiece of the Spirit, and infallible; but at other times they were fallible as men.

Paul therein, they unitedly urged him, by some overt act, to repudiate what they felt must be a slanderous and false accusation against any apostle of Christ.

These apostolic differences show us that those upon whom the Holy Spirit has been outpoured may differ in opinion on external requirements; they also explain the anomaly of every Protestant sect numbering amongst its staunch supporters many pious and sincere-hearted men, each of whom upholds his own church as the true development of the gospel system. The comprehension of all Christians under one form of church government is but of little importance, compared with that of every church being united to the one living Vine, and, as different fruit-bearing branches, deriving all life and nourishment from Him alone. This oneness of root will ever produce an unity which, though it cause not all men to see eye to eye, would prepare them to bear with one another in their differences, and destroy that sectarian bitterness with which Satan, under the guise of zeal for God's truth, has embroiled us.

The early Friends, perceiving great diversity of creeds amongst protestant professors, but finding no solace to their own souls within the pale of any, endeavoured to throw entirely aside the dust and rust which had accumulated during successive ages. They sought in earnest prayer for the guidance and enlightening influence of the Holy Spirit, and in humble dependence thereon they searched and studied those scriptures which "Holy men of old spake as they were moved by the Holy Ghost." So thoroughly, in their estimate, were the traditions and adaptations of unregenerate man interwoven in all religious sects, that many Friends feared a critical study of the bible, lest they should be insensibly drawn away from that in which alone they felt security—viz., the Holy Spirit enlightening the seeking mind to comprehend its truths.

They knew from experience, that no syllogistic or historical belief in the bible could change the heart, or purify the conscience from dead works. They dreaded lest scholastic divinity should substitute, within them, theology in the place of religion;—dry logical proofs of the existence of a God, for that inward objective revelation of Himself upon which their belief was immovably based. Possessed of this positive faith—a faith which in its very nature is unassailable by atheist or sceptic, and commencing with the postulate "God is—because I *feel* Him to be;" they felt that no circumstantial evidences, proofs, or historic doubts, could affect this inward witness for God in the soul. Knowing also that "Except a man be born again he cannot see the kingdom of God," they went forth, unlettered as many of them were, to preach the gospel to every creature—appealing, not to hereditary beliefs or school catechisms, but to that Spirit of Truth within, of which the apostle John declared "He that believeth on the Son of God hath the witness in himself." Their belief in Jesus Christ was built upon this foundation, and they boldly maintained that, not by historical faith or ceremonial observances, but by a heartfelt belief in Him alone, the once crucified and now risen Lord, could man be saved. They maintained that, under the Gospel dispensation, there was by divine grace an inward witness in the soul of every man,\* which recognized as truth, instinc-

---

\* "That true Light which lighteth every man that cometh into the world was the life in the world, and was divine and eternal, and not natural; and wicked men were enlightened by this Light, else how could they hate it, as it is expressly said they did?"—(*Fox, Journal*, p. 362.)

"They that believed in it came out of condemnation to the light of life, and became the children of it; but they that hated it, and did not believe

tively and immediately, many of the New Testament doctrines, and which gave response to that eternal truth which is contained in the lively oracles of God; and that the appeal of the rightly authorized minister to this unbiased inner conscience was direct and irresistible. "By manifestation of the truth, they thus commended themselves and their doctrines to every man's conscience in the sight of God."

The steady maintenance of this principle caused the grossest misrepresentations; Friends were accused of exalting an inward light or principle, in opposition to the Holy Scriptures, of denying the outward coming of our Lord, and of disparaging the letter of Scripture; and many partial quotations from their writings favour these unjust attacks.*

But in the same way as the logical faculty of a man is capable of embracing and recognising mathematical

---

in it, were condemned by it, though they made a profession of Christ."—(*Fox, Journal*, fol. ed., p. 20.)

"Unto all men is a visitation given, and they that do perish it is because they do not believe in Christ; and destruction is of a man's self, but salvation is of God, through believing in his Son, who takes away sin."—(*Edw. Burroughs' Works*, fol. ed., 1672, p. 440.)

* "This most horrid accusation has been answered a thousand times before, by declaring that He that laid down his life, and suffered his body to be crucified by. the Jews, is Christ, the only Son of the Most High God."—(*Penn's Works*, fol. ed., 1726, vol. ii. p. 65.)

"We do not hereby intend any ways to lessen or derogate from the atonement and sacrifice of Jesus Christ; but, on the contrary, do magnify and exalt it. We believe all those things to have been certainly transacted which are recorded in the Holy Scriptures, concerning the birth, life, miracles, sufferings, resurrection and ascension of Christ. Yea, it were damnable unbelief not to believe it."—(*Barclay, Apology*, props. v. and vi. s. 15).

"As certainly as there was a Chief Priest, and Jews, and Pilate there outwardly, so certainly was Christ persecuted by them, and did suffer there outwardly under them."—(*Fox, Journal*, fol. ed., 1765, p. 48. See also Declaration of Faith in next chapter.)

truths which it might be quite unable to originate; or as the mind perceives the harmony and beauty of poetic thought, when placed before it, which it could never have struck out for itself—thoughts which "lie dormant or nebulous until the creative voice of genius condenses and shapes them for us into distinct forms"—so also is there a witness implanted in the original structure of the soul, which, though extinguished under the fall, is renewed under the gospel, and which, though it has no capacity to discover new truth, does respond to, and is in harmony with, that which the Scriptures reveal. Appealing to this alone, they cared neither for logic nor syllogism; but, discrediting all human calculations as to how the soul of man could most effectually be reached, they preached, like Peter of old, "in the ability that God giveth." A similar effect followed; their hearers, recognising the truth when thus proclaimed with power, were pricked in their hearts, crying out, "Men and brethren, what must we do to be saved?" It was from no lack of historic knowledge\* that these converts had remained dead in trespasses and sins, but the Holy Spirit now carried the word from the lips of the preachers to the hearts of the hearers, and multitudes flocked to the spiritual standard thus erected.†

---

\* "There are two kinds of faith. The one says, I believe because good men have told me so. The other, I believe because God hath visited me by His love, and given me an assurance therein that He is my Saviour."—(*Stephen Crisp*).

† "What is the difference between Paul's faith and the faith of professing Christendom? They believed in Christ Himself as their risen and ever-living Saviour; instead of which, do we not, in this nineteenth century, direct our belief towards the circumstances of His incarnation, His life, death, or resurrection, and take these as the objects of faith, instead of Him in whom they all centre. We believe in certain facts, instead of seeking to be brought into a living faith in the Son of God, Jesus *my* Saviour, in whom all the facts unite."—(*Fragments, &c.*)

The Friends explicitly and continually declared that, like Luther and the sixteenth century reformers, they had no new doctrines to advance, but only a renewing of the old ones. R. Barclay states (*Apology*, prop. iii. s. 9): "So we distinguish betwixt a revelation of a new gospel and new doctrines, and a new revelation of the good old gospel and doctrines; the last we plead for, but the first we utterly deny." Again (*Apology*, prop. x. s. 12): "We need not miracles, because we preach no new gospel, but that which is already confirmed by all the miracles of Christ and his apostles, and we offer nothing but that which we are ready and able to confirm by the testimony of the Scriptures."

## CHAPTER II.

#### FUNDAMENTAL DOCTRINES.

I cannot set forth the tenets of the Friends better than by the following extracts from the declaration of faith, published, in 1671, by George Fox and others:—*

"Whereas many scandalous lies and slanders have been cast upon us to render us odious; as that we deny God and Christ Jesus and the Scriptures of truth, &c., we do plainly and sincerely declare:

"That we do own and believe in the only wise, omnipotent, and everlasting God, the Creator of all things both in heaven and in earth, and the preserver of all that He hath made; who is God over all, blessed for ever.

"And we own and believe in Jesus Christ, His beloved and only begotten Son, in whom He is well pleased; who was conceived by the Holy Ghost, and born of the Virgin Mary; in whom we have redemption through His blood, even the forgiveness of sins; who is the express image of the invisible God, the first-born of every creature, by whom were all things created that are in heaven and in earth. And we own and believe that He was made a sacrifice for sin, who knew no sin; that He was crucified for us in the flesh, without

---

\* This confession of faith was addressed to the Governor of Barbadoes. It has been frequently reprinted by authority of the London Yearly Meeting, and forms part of the preface to their Book of Discipline, published in 1834.

the gates of Jerusalem; and that He was buried, and rose again the third day by the power of his Father, for our justification; and that He ascended up into heaven, and now sitteth at the right hand of God.

"This Jesus, who was the foundation of the holy prophets and apostles, is our foundation; and we believe that there is no other foundation to be laid than that is laid, even Christ Jesus; who tasted death for every man, shed his blood for all men, and is the propitiation for our sins, and not for ours only, but also for the sins of the whole world; according as John the Baptist testified of Him, when he said, 'Behold the Lamb of God, which taketh away the sins of the world' (John i. 29). We believe that He alone is our Redeemer and Saviour, even the Captain of our salvation; who saves us from sin, as well as from hell and the wrath to come, and destroys the devil and his works; He is the seed of the woman that bruises the serpent's head, to wit, Christ Jesus, the Alpha and Omega, the First and the Last. He is (as the Scriptures of truth say of Him) our wisdom and righteousness, justification and redemption; neither is there salvation in any other, for 'there is no other name under heaven given among men whereby we may be saved, and He is the Shepherd and Bishop of our souls.'

"He it is that is now come in the Spirit, and hath given us an understanding that we may know Him that is true. He rules in our hearts by His law of love and of life, and makes us free from the law of sin and death. We have no life but by Him; for He is the quickening Spirit, the second Adam, the Lord from heaven, by whose blood we are cleansed, and our consciences sprinkled from dead works to serve the living God. He is our Mediator, that makes peace between God offended and us offending; He being the oath of God, the New Covenant of light, life, grace, and peace; the author and finisher of our faith. This Lord Jesus Christ, the Heavenly Man, the Emmanuel, God with us, we all own and believe in; Him whom the high priest raged against, and said He had spoken blasphemy; whom the priests and the elders of the Jews took counsel together against, and put to death; the same whom Judas betrayed for thirty pieces of silver.—This we say is that Lord Jesus Christ whom we own to be our life and salvation.

"Concerning the Holy Scriptures, we do believe that they were given forth by the Holy Spirit of God, through the holy men of God, who (as the Scripture itself declares (2 Peter i. 21), 'spake as they were moved by the Holy Ghost.' We believe they are to be read, believed, and fulfilled (he that fulfils them is Christ); and they are 'profitable for doctrine, for reproof, for correction, and for instruction in righteousness, that the man of God may be perfect, throughly furnished unto all good works' (2 Tim. iii. 16); and are 'able to make wise unto salvation, through faith in Christ Jesus.' We believe that the Holy Scriptures are the words of God; for it is said (Exod. xx.), 'God spake all these words, saying,' &c., meaning the ten commandments given forth upon Mount Sinai. So we call the Holy Scriptures, as Christ and the Apostles called them, and holy men of God called them—viz., the words of God."

Founded upon the Apostle's creed, "If thou shalt confess with thy mouth the Lord Jesus, and shalt believe in thine heart that God hath raised him from the dead, thou shalt be saved," the Friends took their stand upon these two essentials to salvation; viz., a heart belief in Jesus as the alone Mediator between God and man, and an open acknowledgment of this belief before all the world. The main distinctions between them and others were—

1stly. Upon the immediate teaching of the Holy Spirit.

2ndly. Upon all types and outward ordinances being abolished under the gospel.

3rdly. In their form of worship, and appointment of ministers.

4thly. In their manner of carrying out into daily life and practice the commands of our Lord.

Believing that the New Testament contained all needful instructions for the forming of churches or congregations of believers, they took this as the basis of order and discipline as a society; but they regarded the Holy Spirit, the Comforter, as the ordained means whereby each member may know his *individual* path of duty. Banishing all preconceived notions and practices, and with their own wills and thoughts kept in subjection unto this Spirit of Truth, which, saith Christ, "proceedeth from the Father, and shall testify of me," they sought to restore and place again before the world that faith once delivered to the saints.

The fact of Christianity having been upheld by temporal power and splendour for 1300 years, was to them no proof that our Saviour so commanded it. The institution of distinct orders of priests and laymen, and the dogma of a college education as a necessary routine for all ministers of Christ, was no evidence to them of the soundness of these un-apostolic practices. In like manner the laws compelling attendance at the parish church, tithes, a salaried ministry, a musical form of worship, set forms of prayer,* the general adoption of water bap-

---

\* It is a striking fact that under the Mosaic dispensation no forms of prayer whatever were instituted. All supplications arose spontaneously

tism, and of the Lord's supper, as external rites,* the custom of judicial swearing, of Christian professors engaging in war, of keeping their fellow-men in slavery, or of living a worldly life, gave no evidence to these Friends that such things were necessarily in accordance with the will of God.

Disregarding traditions and customs, they went straight to the New Testament, to see what was therein ordained by Christ, or commanded in the inspired writings of his Apostles; and whilst pointing to the light that enlighteneth every man, as that by which each must individually be guided, yet in no instance during their many disputes and controversies with others, did they appeal to any standard but that of the Holy Scriptures, as the rule of faith and practice which must govern all the followers of Christ.†

---

out of the special occasions which drew them forth, and their origin was a sense of individual necessities and of God's blessings. If this was the case in a religious system which, in its minutest forms and particulars, was all ordained of God, it can scarcely be maintained that the same sense of need of divine blessing is insufficient under the Gospel for the exercise of heartfelt prayer without any set forms.

* Sprinkling was substituted for immersion about the middle of the third century, and the baptism of infants about the same period. (See Cave's *Primitive Christianity,* and Neander's *History.*) The baptism, through sponsors, &c., of dead men, of unborn infants, as well as of inanimate things, such as bells, followed the age of Augustine.—(*Lawson's Baptismologia,* ed. 1703.) The consecration of churches was unknown until the time of Constantine (*vide* Cave); and tithes, though first suggested at the end of the fourth century, were not made compulsory until the age of Charlemagne. —(*Hallam's Middle Ages,* cap. vii.)

† "With this argument I shall try you all. Whatsoever is professed and practised for religion, for which there is neither command nor precedent in Scripture, is not according to the Scripture; let this fall where it may, it is truth; and therefore let all people come to trial, and receive your judgment by this rule."—(*E. Burroughs' Works,* fo. ed. p. 326.)

"We ever choose to express our belief of the Christian faith and doc-

This is worthy of special notice; for, though objecting to every usage which the New Testament did not warrant, and at the same time testifying to the continuance of that same guidance which existed in the days of the Apostles, and was promised unto all future believers, they never assumed this latter as the touchstone by which doctrine was to be tested. To the Law and to the Testimony, was their language to all opposers.

Barclay (*Apology*, prop. iii.), states, that they (the Scriptures) contain a full and ample account of all the chief principles of the doctrine of Christ held forth in divers precious declarations and exhortations, which by the moving of God's Spirit were spoken and written unto the churches, &c.; but that being a declaration of the fountain, and not the fountain itself,* they are subordinate to the Spirit of God that gave them forth. Their primary belief in the inspired volume being grounded not on critical evidences, but on its accordance with the intimations and wants of a regenerate nature, the Friends considered also that the truths which it contains could be comprehended only by the enlightening aid of that Spirit by which they were given forth; for "the natural man receiveth not the things of the Spirit of God; for they are foolishness unto him: neither can he know them, because they are spiritually discerned." (1 Cor. ii. 14). It was, nevertheless, a clearly recognised doctrine of the

---

trine in the terms of Holy Scripture, and reject all principles and doctrines whatsoever that are repugnant thereunto."—(*Penn's Works*, fo. ed., vol. ii. p. 878.) In all of George Fox's controversies with priests and others, the New Testament was the standard appealed to, and he very frequently preached and disputed bible in hand.

* We may know the Scriptures, but do we know Him of whom they testify? They tell us of a city of habitation prepared for us, and they tell us of the way to it; but they are neither the way nor the city. (*Fragments, &c.* p. 72.)

Friends, that "whatsoever any do, pretending to the Spirit, which is contrary to the Scriptures, shall be accounted and reckoned a delusion of the devil." (Barclay, *Apology*, prop. x. s. 6).

The doctrine of the inward guidance of the Holy Spirit, which they felt called upon especially to promulgate, is theoretically admitted by most Christians,[*] but much difference exists in their views of the mode in which its operations are perceived. As already stated, the Friends held that the Holy Spirit, the Comforter, doth make his voice known to the humble believer, and if faithfully obeyed and followed, He will lead into a true conformity with the will of God, both in temporal and spiritual things; but they knew, from painful experience, that the flesh was weak, and that they too often followed their own wills and Satan's devices, in preference to that which was the will of God concerning them. Thus, whilst the Scriptures clearly portray the faith by which we must be saved, and the way in which the disciples of Christ must

---

[*] "To those, lastly, who cannot help seeing that the doctrine of Christ in every man, as the indwelling word of God, the light who lights every one who comes into the world, is no peculiar tenet of the Quakers, but one which runs through the whole of the Old and New Testaments, and without which they would both be unintelligible, just as the same doctrine runs through the whole history of the early church for the first two centuries, and is the only explanation of them. To all these this noble little book will recommend itself."—(*Kingsley's Preface to Theologica Germanica*, p. 7.)

"We know the Spirit of God is present with us by the effects which he produces in us." "He is lodged in our very essence, and is a soul within the soul, to irradiate its understanding, rectify its will, purify its passions, and enliven all the powers of man."—(*Addison*).

"The further a man advances in holiness, the more capable he is rendered by the illumination of the Holy Spirit of distinguishing what proceeds from the Holy Spirit, and what from the flesh, and of discerning all the disturbing influences of the latter."—(*Neander's Planting of Christianity*, p. 470.)

ever walk, they point also to the law of God written in the heart, by which our individual path is to be known. "The steps of a good man are ordered of the Lord;" and his spiritual guidance, they maintained, was clear, immediate, and perceptible.

Many misapprehensions have arisen, both within and without the pale of the Society, from the confused terms and phrases employed by Friends in relation to the inward light. Their doctrine has ever been, that "as in Adam all die, even so in Christ shall all be made alive;" that whilst there is, by nature, a power constantly drawing man down into sin and perdition, so also there is, by grace, in every man, a light shining in this darkness, which causes remorse and sense of guilt for sins committed, although this light may be dimmed, and even extinguished, by a long career of depravity. If man is by nature "dead in trespasses and sins," that within him which reproves sin and condemns it, cannot arise from his own sin-loving and dead nature, but must be divine in its origin. Christ, by his death, condemned sin in the flesh, and by his resurrection justifies all them that believe.

The development of their views on the spirituality of Christ's kingdom affected so greatly the practices of Friends, that it seems needful to examine the reasons advanced in their justification. The more so, as, if unsound, it would greatly affect the solution of the question before us. The Friends maintained that our Saviour came to fulfil or consummate the Mosaic law, and to abolish all symbols and shadows, all Jewish types, sacrificial ordinances, and priesthood; ("which stood only in meats and drinks, and 'divers washings, and carnal ordinances, imposed on them until the time of reformation,'") and to introduce their antitypes or spiritual realities. "When he (our Saviour) cometh into the world, he saith, Lo, I come to do thy will, O God. He taketh away the first (or typical), that he may establish the second (or spiritual)." (Heb. x.) The Society of Friends held that under the Christian dispensation God must be worshipped in the spirit, (inwardly, not at Jerusalem or Mount Gerizim); and in truth (not by shadows); that our Lord Jesus Christ never inculcated any special or new outward ceremonies, to be applicable to Gentile converts, although he sought to give a new meaning to those Jewish practices under which his hearers had been educated, and to the continuance of many of which they so tenaciously clung, both before and after the day of Pentecost.

John expressly declared (in contradistinction to the water baptism which was a common outward recognition amongst Jewish proselytes in that day\*—a

\* This fact has been disputed; but the proselytes were of two descriptions: "proselytes of the gate," who forsook idolatry and worshipped the true God, but did not conform to the Jewish law; and proselytes of Justice, who went further, and embraced the whole legal and ceremonial system. According to the learned Maimonides, it was the latter only who were baptized, and the ceremony took place about three days after that of circumcision. It was done like that of John, by immersion; and after a promise of faithful adherence to the Jewish institutions into which by this ceremony the convert was admitted, he became a complete Jew, and as a new or regenerate man.—(*Issure Biah*, cap. 13, 14; *Selden, de Synedriis*, lib. i. cap. 3.)

Lightfoot also informs us that, according to the tradition of the Rabbins, circumcision, baptism, and sacrifice, were enjoined on every male, and the two latter on every female, convert from heathenism to the Jewish faith. It was an acknowledged axiom, he further states, that no man could be a proselyte until he was circumcised and baptized. Again, the Babylonish Gemara (part of the Talmud) contains a disputation upon this question between certain Rabbis, which, after arguments *pro* and *con*, concludes thus:—He is no proselyte until he be both circumcised and baptized. Paul's fearing lest he should be accused of baptizing in *his own name* also proves the prevalence of this custom amongst teachers of new doctrines.

baptism which he himself administered "unto repentance")—" He shall baptize you with the Holy Ghost;" words which are emphatically repeated by each evangelist. This difference was again clearly marked out by our Saviour (Acts i. 5): "For John truly baptized with water, but ye shall be baptized with the Holy Ghost." The symbolical contrast between the baptism of John (by water) and that of Christ (by fire) is very striking, and leads to the impression that John considered fire, and not water, as the symbol of the new dispensation. Now, since Jesus Christ in no case administered water baptism (John iv. 2), (although he suffered his disciples to do so to the Jewish followers), and since his disciples were never baptized with water in the name of the Trinity (unless we are to imagine they baptized one another), it is clear that the only baptism ministered by Christ is that of the Holy Ghost.

When the Apostle speaks of the "like *antitype*, (marg. reading) even baptism, which doth now save us," he describes it as being an internal thing—"The answer of a good conscience towards God." It is with this construction that the Friends understand the words, "Whoso believeth and is baptized shall be saved"—a heartfelt belief and a conscience purified as by fire. But even taken in a literal sense, as is usually done, and remembering also that baptism was practised before the Christian era, and therefore not instituted or originated by our Saviour, this text and other similar ones\* appear

\* The command, "Go ye and baptize all nations into the name of the Father, the Son, and the Holy Ghost" (if taken literally), gives a new and wider direction to an old and well-understood Jewish ceremony. The emphatic words are, *all nations*, not Jews only; and the *new faith*—the Father, the Son, and the Holy Ghost. The condition of Apollos and disciples living at Ephesus exemplifies this view. They declared "they had not so much as heard whether there be any Holy Ghost." They had

to indicate only that needful outward confession which existed amongst proselytes of all kinds when they changed their faith, and is therefore synonymous with the Apostle's declaration, "Whoso confesseth with the mouth," &c., "shall be saved." The word baptism was a short term understood by all Jews as signifying outward profession of adhesion to a new faith. The Friends therefore held that the only saving baptism is that of the Holy Ghost; but that the Redeemer, as in many other instances, allowed his Jewish disciples to adopt that external mode of confession, which they and the scribes and Rabbis would most clearly understand, but which He never adopted himself.

A similar explanation applies to the ceremony of the Lord's supper. Friends regarded its observance by Jewish disciples and others, not as commanded by Christ, but permissible to those who also, in their observance of circumcision, purifyings, &c., clung to the Mosaic ritual. This opinion is strongly confirmed by the fact that Matthew and John, who were both disciples and ear-witnesses of all that passed, would undoubtedly have expressed it in clear terms, had they understood that any new ordinance was established by our Lord; but neither they nor Mark, who gives a minute account of these events, have any allusion whatever to the perpetuity of any ceremony. Luke only, who was not an apostle, reports the words which have

been baptized unto the faith of John, and were afterwards baptized unto the faith of Jesus—the ceremony would appear to have been the same in both cases, but its object very different. The command to baptize is recorded only by Matthew; and being accompanied by the power, "Lo, I am with you alway," seems to point to the one baptism of Christ which should be administered through them. Is not this meaning more consonant with all His other spiritual teachings, than to suppose that our Saviour's last words instituted a type instead of a reality?

been so construed. The inference therefore is, that John, Matthew, and Mark, as inspired evangelists, themselves regarded the words spoken by our Lord, "This do in remembrance of me," as applicable only to the feast then being celebrated, and they consequently omitted them in their narration (a course of acting which would have been utterly impossible for these three inspired evangelists to have adopted, had *they* understood the words as a command binding on all future ages). The love-feasts of the early Christians were of quite a different character; and the great question between Friends and others is not, Are such things expedient or comforting? but rather, Is any outward rite, new or old, specially commanded by our Saviour as binding on all his followers? The only distinct new command was that of washing one another's feet; yet, by applying to this the same test that Friends apply to baptism and the Eucharist — viz., the Christian religion is not ceremonial — all protestants give it a figurative interpretation, and decline to perpetuate the form. If the non-binding nature of these ceremonies be admitted, the Friends have every justification on the grounds of expediency. The conscientious abstaining therefrom has never stood in the way of any single person so travelling his heavenward journey; but their adoption has led millions to rely upon baptismal regeneration, confession, the real presence, and extreme unction, instead of a heartfelt saving knowledge of Christ.

The spiritual truths symbolized by these types were what Friends sought after and lived in.* They deeply

---

\* In a paper entitled "Gospel Truths," and signed by William Penn, Thomas Story, and others, they state, "We believe the necessity of the one baptism of Christ, as well as of his one supper which he promiseth to eat

felt that, unless washed by Christ himself, they had no part with him, and that unless they became so entirely incorporated with Him as to partake of that true spiritual feasting upon Jesus, whereof he himself declares, "Except ye eat the flesh of the Son of man, and drink his blood, ye have no life in you," they could not be amongst the number of those who, having seen the Son, and believed on Him, shall have everlasting life, and be raised up at the last day.

The same deep-rooted convictions on the reality of religion led George Fox and his cotemporaries to uphold the spiritual nature of gospel worship. Knowing also the tendency there is in the mind of man to stop short at the symbol, or, in other words, to transfer to the visible sign the feelings due alone to the thing signified, they dreaded the introduction of anything not commanded in the New Testament, which, from its adaptation to the æsthetic emotions rather than to the religious feelings, might draw the eye of faith away from the Invisible, or produce that semi-sensuous delight in a religious worship imposingly conducted with a tasteful ceremonial, which may exist without any true reverential love towards God, or for the essence and inner spirit of religion. A devotional feeling may be produced by the glory of the setting sun, the sublimity of the ocean, or the majesty of night, without any drawing out of the soul towards God our Saviour.

Friends were also, above all things, anxious that no man-made or needless interventions should obtrude between the soul of the worshipper and the infinitely holy

with those who open the door of their heart unto Him; being the baptism and supper signified by outward signs; which though we disuse, we judge not those that conscientiously practise them."—(Penn's Works, vol. i. p. 756.)

object of its adoration; and protested against the worship of a whole congregation being dependent upon the presence or absence of any man.

So strong is the temptation to embody our inmost feelings in forms tangible or visible, that all religions are affected by it. The hugeness of the Ninevite and Egyptian gods, the beauty of the Grecian and the grotesqueness of the Indian idols, are all evidences of this universal tendency to materialize spirit. The process by which many Romanists have, through temples, crosses, images, and sacred relics, gradually sunk into an idolizing of the symbols themselves, is similar to that through which paganism must have passed, from the original worship of one God,—to, firstly, that of the works which reveal His power, and downwards, finally, into the adoration of stocks and stones, the work of men's hands.

Not only is this so, but, even in worldly things, the mind inclines to estimate, for its own sake, that by which pleasure or comfort is procurable, but which has no value apart from what it instrumentally can effect. To illustrate this we may point to the love of money which haunts an avaricious man. In the first place he loves it because of the gratifications which he can thereby purchase; then he values the thing itself for its own sake, and the process goes on, until finally he cares nothing for the end for which he originally sought wealth, viz., corporeal ease and luxuries; but his thoughts are intent upon hoarding that which is consequently to him not only utterly worthless, but is greatly adding to his anxieties. So also with religion;—the same tendency exists to love the forms and rituals themselves, and for their own sake, and gradually to lose sight of that on account of which alone such forms were adopted.

The Friends held also that the spirituality of religion

could be most effectually maintained by having no outward ritual or form of worship, and that God alone can call and prepare for the true ministry of the gospel; that, as the prophet or teacher of the Old Testament was sent of God, to teach and to preach unto His people, so now is the office of the Christian prophet the same; being taught of God to declare His will to man.

The duty of prophets and prophetesses, under the old dispensation, was not connected with any sacrifices or ceremonial rites which pertained to the order of priesthood;[*] but they were to rouse the spiritual feelings of those they addressed, sometimes by foretelling future trials and troubles, but more often by exhortation only; also to keep in the remembrance of their hearers that Saviour who was to come. Although the gift of foretelling future events is no longer needed, yet all their other spiritual gifts of exhortation, warning, instruction, and reproof, and pointing to the "King who reigneth in righteousness," are needed now as much or more than they ever were, and the Christian preacher of this day might almost adopt the very same language.

We know that the ancient prophets were men liable to err, and of like passions with others. It is evident also that the Christian prophets were not infallible exponents of truth, since the Apostle Paul directs others to judge of what was said (1 Cor. xiv.), and he further adds, "For ye may all prophesy, one by one, that all may learn, and that all may be comforted." The spirits of the prophets were to be subject to the prophets, clearly because, being only human instruments, Paul could not regard them as perfect organs of the spirit. This remark applies exactly to the views with which ministers amongst Friends are regarded.

[*] Vide also Rev. Scott Surtees on "The Ministry of the Word."

The gift of ministry is committed unto them; but it also follows that this treasure, being in earthen vessels, may often be stained and corrupted thereby.

The Levitical priesthood was *hereditary*, and was instituted, not for instructing the people, or warning them against sin and idolatry, but to attend at the altar until, by the one eternal High Priest, their appointment was for ever abolished. We find, however, that the prophets were called from various tribes, and of different worldly occupations,—as Elisha from the plough, and Amos from the dressing of vines. So also in the apostolic churches, the learned Paul, the eloquent Apollos, and the devoted Timothy, were preachers neither from college education nor apostolic succession, but primarily because God called them as individuals, and sent them forth to preach the word; their qualifications were, the gift of preaching bestowed upon them, and obedience in its faithful exercise. Peter (Acts ii. 18) expressly points to the increase, and not to the diminution, of prophecy under the gospel dispensation.—" On my servants, and on my handmaidens I will pour out in those days of my spirit, and they shall prophesy." Friends therefore maintained that as in the Mosaic dispensation men and women of every occupation were called to this work,* as in the time of

---

\* That women both prayed and prophesied in the early churches is evident from Scripture, and from the instructions given by Paul (1 Cor. ii. 4 and 5) as to how men and women should each conduct themselves whilst so doing; neither is this at variance to the command, that "women should keep silence in the churches," and not "teach or usurp authority over the man." Locke (*Epistles of St. Paul*, p. 137) states : " The women in the churches were not to assume the personage of doctors, or speak there as teachers,—this carried with it the appearance of superiority, and was forbidden ; not even to ask questions in the church—this signified equality, and was also forbidden. But this subordination to man, which God, for order's sake, had instituted in the world, hindered not but that He might make use of the weaker sex to an extraordinary function, whenever He thought fit."

the Apostles the same thing existed, so in these latter days, wherein we stand more than ever in need of this continued outpouring of the Spirit, the gift of prophecy, or preaching the word, is still bestowed. The setting apart, the selection, and the preparation of all true ministers, must be of Christ, who giveth to every man severally as He will.

In harmony with this system of plurality of preachers, the Friends regarded congregational silent waiting upon God as the true form of gospel worship. By it not only are the souls of individuals refreshed, but an unity of spirit is felt to interflow amongst its participators, and the living ministry has, as in the Apostle's days, proper opportunity for expression.

There is no probability that the Apostles either wrote prayers for the use of the churches, or composed any formal hymns of praise for the help of others;* neither is it likely that any instrumental music was used when the believers assembled together in the synagogue, or in an "upper chamber," or when they went into temples and theatres for teaching and preaching. It was upon the gathering together in His name, and not upon any particular acts when gathered, that the Redeemer's promise was bestowed—" There am I in the midst of them." A state of abstractedness from worldly thoughts; the prostration of our own selves, soul and will, before an infinite God; and the holding communion with Him through the Holy Spirit the Comforter, Friends considered the appointed means for Christian worship, and that in it alone could the spontaneous language of praise, prayer, and exhortation be freely offered.

* The earliest hymns of St. Hilary and others were not written until the fourth century, at which period also a choir of singers was first introduced.

Much more might be said upon this and the preceding subjects, if space permitted. Less would hardly suffice upon that which forms the basis of church-fellowship.

My object has been not so much to combat arguments advanced against these views, as to prove the Scripture grounds upon which they stand, and to shew that there is nothing unsound which must cause declension in numbers or vitality.

## CHAPTER III.

**TESTIMONIES.**

Much difference of opinion exists respecting the particular way in which Christian testimonies are to be borne before the world, but there is a general theoretic assent as to what the New Testament declares these to be.

Although the practice of Friends is in many respects different, I do not find that any distinct line of demarcation can be drawn between it and that of the sincerehearted of other denominations. As already observed, there is a great variety in mental constitution, and different minds have ever developed the same principle in different ways, according to what each felt to be most consistent with the object to be accomplished. I will, therefore, briefly enumerate those testimonies which the Friends consider to have been committed to them as a Society to uphold; and afterwards investigate how far their means of effecting this have been suitable or adapted to the present age.

It will be generally admitted that national feelings, notions, and habits, must shape the manner in which we impart our sentiments to others. A costume which is reasonable in one country, is ludicrous if adopted in another; and a mode of paying respect here, may be disrespectful elsewhere. To the initiated, the sign represents the thing it signifies, but to others it may be meaningless; and the three-cornered hat, long stockings, and shoe-buckles of a consistent Friend sixty years since, would convey no more religious idea to a Hindoo or Turk, than would the costume of a Chelsea pensioner. The dress of a Christian woman, or plain Friend, of this age, would have appeared highly indecorous and unbecoming to the Jewish ideas of Paul and Peter; neither would the robe and sandals of the latter be a respectable and sensible attire for an English Christian.* So also the bending of the body, or the removing of the hat, as practised by English courtiers, would not be respectful amongst the Siamese, with whom prostration is the ordinary way of expressing obeisance. The intent of the Gospel was to purify the heart.—" Cleanse first that which is within the cup and the platter, that the outside of them may be clean also." If we make the tree good, there will be a similarity in the kind of fruit produced, but there need not be a perfect uniformity in its appearance.

George Fox and his cotemporaries believed that God was to be glorified by every man, in whatever position of life he might be placed; and that the courtier or statesman, tradesman or mechanic, prince or peasant, was each able, by honestly following his individual calling, to magnify the name of the Almighty. This appears a slight thing to acknowledge; but it is nevertheless

* An attempt was made by the early Christians to carry the badge of their religious profession upon their dress, by wearing a cross attached to the ordinary national costume. This being applicable to all nations, and conveying a distinct idea, would seem an open and justifiable mode of declaring their faith; but when we reflect that out of this simple act arose charms, relics, and rosaries, and a superstitious feeling bordering on idolatry; that people prided themselves upon this outward cross-bearing as being in itself meritorious; and worst of all, when we see that this emblem of a crucified Saviour is, in the guise of curious and costly ornaments, made to pander to the vainest love of dress and worldly display, it suggests that any attempt to convey to others, by dress, the feelings which animate a community, is very dangerous in practice.

the greatest practical problem of life,—so to follow our various avocations, that in doing our daily work we may add to the glory of God.—"Not slothful in business; fervent in spirit, serving the Lord." Whilst many regarded a secluded or monastic life as the best suited to the growth of religion in the soul, and others considered certain orders, such as Jesuits, priests, clergy, and divines, as the highest forms of spirituality, George Fox promulgated the loftier Scripture doctrine, that all may become priests unto God (Rev. i. 6); and that whether as fisherman or tent-maker, male or female, each might follow his own business; and whilst daily doing his duty "in that state of life unto which it has pleased God to call him," might also be appointed by the one Great Head, to fill any and every office in his militant church.

The holding of any spiritual gift being thus compatible with common worldly avocations, it also followed, that any occupation, which in its nature would exclude these gifts, was not lawful for a Christian professor, however plausible or lucrative it might be. Being thoroughly satisfied, from experience, as well as from Scripture testimony, that whilst honestly engaged in supporting themselves and their families by daily toil, their souls might be hourly nourished by divine grace, they endeavoured to "acknowledge God in all their ways." The commands, "Seek ye first the Kingdom of God and His righteousness, and all these things shall be added unto you;" and "Whether ye eat or drink, or whatsoever ye do, do all to the glory of God;" were considered literally binding upon every individual member; and in the selection of a business, of the locality in which they settled, as well as in the choice of associates, and in marriage engagements, the first thing to be considered was not, Will it conduce to my worldly position or happiness? but, Will it draw me closer unto God? This was a fundamental rule ; and, to keep it and other similar duties constantly in remembrance, annual epistles were issued by the body.

During the first period of their existence, this law was faithfully maintained and practised by the Society at large, as it still is by many of its members. I do not say that with many sincere-hearted Christians under every denomination this same care does not exist; but I know of no community wherein it is so prominently insisted on as amongst the Friends, or in which it has been so conscientiously carried out. Any pursuit or amusement upon which, as dependent children, they could not ask God's blessing, and for which, when enjoyed, they could not return Him thanks, was regarded as unfit for a Christian to indulge in. Under this feeling, many ordinary pleasures were foregone, such as profuse entertainments, frivolous reading, concerts, balls. and other like recreations. By taking up the daily cross, they strove to obey the injunction of the Apostle, and in "denying ungodliness and worldly lusts, to live soberly, righteously, and godly."

The effects of thus testing all worldly engagements by their harmony with a life of faith were strikingly exemplified. With such a guiding principle, it is no marvel that the integrity and honesty of a Quaker soon became proverbial. They became very prosperous in outward circumstances ; and in thousands of instances they have proved that all the relations of life, the duties of citizenship, and engagements in worldly occupation, are compatible with the highest spiritual gifts and church offices, and a life of devotedness unto God.

The next governing principle in their system has been,

"Do unto others as ye would that they should do unto you." This law not only excluded defamation of character, but forbad their taking advantage of the ignorance, obstinacy, or foolishness of their neighbour, or advancing their own interests at another's expense; it led to a toleration of the opinions and practices, as well as the amelioration of the woes, of others; to the abolition of slavery, and many other like consequences. It affords also the mainspring to the philanthropic efforts with which the Friends have been so nobly connected, and is the basis which underlies their political sentiments. How far their deductions are sound and logical I need not investigate; but the standard by which, as a body, their decisions are governed, is one not of expediency, but of the law of justice and right. Considering the freedom and independence of judgment which is encouraged amongst them, their views on all political questions are on this account arrived at with great unanimity.

The testimony on self-denial is equally prominent with those already alluded to.—" If meat make my brother to offend, I will eat no flesh while the world standeth." The loving one's neighbour as oneself, required them to forego things lawful in themselves, but which, in practical operation, led other souls astray. Their objections to music, theatrical entertainments, hunting or shooting, to a high cultivation of the fine arts, and in many instances latterly to the use of alcoholic drinks, were mainly founded upon the conviction that the abstaining from lawful indulgence, for the sake of a weak brother, was required of them; and that, as a religious body, they ought to discountenance the use of all things which, " though lawful, were not expedient."

Their testimony against war was based upon its clear

antagonism to the commands of our Saviour, and to the Gospel of love and peace.* Whilst other sects mystified their consciences by distinctions of offensive and defensive, provoked and unprovoked, warfare, they went to the root of the matter, and protested against any man being trained in the art of killing a fellow-creature, and boldly declared that they would abide the consequences of this obedience to the law of Christ.

Their objections to all oaths arose from what they considered the command of our Lord, and from the declarations of Christian men needing no appeal to Heaven for confirmation. "Swear not at all; but let your communication be yea, yea, and nay, nay." Out of this same testimony to simplicity of language arose many of the peculiarities by which Friends have been distinguished. "Putting away lying, speak every man truth with his neighbour," implied with them, not merely the absence of direct falsehood, but a truthfulness in action as well as in word. "Plainness of speech" meant truthfulness in impression conveyed, as well as in expression adopted. They considered that all flattering titles were as injurious to the spiritual sensibility of those who used them as of those who received them—that the eulogistic inscriptions erected over the dead, as well as the deceitful language often

* Although Paul declared the Christian warfare to be spiritual and not carnal, and many of the early Christians refused to fight, a sad falling away occurred before and after the era of Constantine. This was consummated finally by the preaching of Peter the Hermit (powerfully seconded by Pope Urban II.), and none doubted but that wicked men who perished in these "Holy Wars" received the reward of martyrdom. Hallam (*Middle Ages*, cap. i.) states: "So many crimes and so much misery have seldom been accumulated in so short a space as in the three years of the first crusade. Cotemporary writers estimate the loss of Christians alone at nearly a million, but at the least computation it must have exceeded half that number."

made use of in addressing the living, were to be alike protested against; and also that the use of the plural number in speaking to a single individual was a practice which had its origin in flattery and pride, and was therefore not right for them to adopt. This same carefulness in speech caused them to object to the heathen names by which the months and days of the week were distinguished, lest they should thus perpetuate an idolatrous feeling.

"Plainness of behaviour" meant an absence of everything that was false in manner, or which would convey an idea either of esteem or respect which was not really felt. This scruple forbad their offering to men certain external marks of reverence, such as bending the knee and uncovering the head, which they considered as due to the Almighty alone.

"Plainness of apparel" signified the simplicity of external appearance by which a Christian should be distinguished from a man of fashion, and the absence of all that would be likely to add to the vanity of the wearer. Its original design was not to give rise to a sectarian costume, but as an outward profession of faith before the world. By thus appealing to the two senses of mankind which can alone take cognizance of inward feeling—viz., to the eye by dress and to the ear by language, there could at no time be any question whether they professed to belong to the kingdom of God, or to that of the world.

The non-observance of fast-days and holy-days, the refusal to pay church-rates and tithes, and their objections to everything which would make religion compulsory, all arose out of the general principles that the types of outward fasts and feasts are superseded by spiritual antitypes—that all days should, under the

Gospel, be kept holy unto the Lord—and that it is not the province of any State to dictate the forms in which the Almighty is to be worshipped by its citizens.

In looking at these testimonies, it must, I think, be acknowledged, that the *spirit* of every one of them is in accordance with the New Testament; and we find that the most serious amongst every class of protestant Christians uphold the same principles as binding upon their own consciences, although many consider that the Friends were needlessly strict, and went a little too far in literally carrying them into practice.

If this explanation be correct, there does not seem to be in these principles anything unsound or unscriptural, which could account for the decline of the Society. On the contrary, as the fullest development of the two great commandments, "Thou shalt love the Lord thy God with all thy heart, and thy neighbour as thyself," they contain the certain elements of endurance, and of ultimate universal adoption.

How far the reader may unite with these conclusions, I know not; but to my own mind the conviction is strong, that neither in origin, nor in fundamental doctrines, nor in principles of action, can any inherent source of decay be detected. All are based upon the same immutable foundation; and having ascertained that the inside is clean, and the sources of action pure, (however much the outside may be corroded), we may turn to those extraneous causes, which are unitedly combining to diminish this Society, whilst they are powerless in checking the progress of its principles.

## CHAPTER IV.

### STATISTICS.

Before pointing out the obstructions to which the spread of Quakerism has been subjected, a few statistical observations appear desirable.

It may seem singular that a religious community, so methodical and thoroughly organised, should not have any numerical records; but at their origin the Friends had no formal act of admission into church membership, and all who united in their Christian testimonies and form of worship, were considered as belonging to the body.

Whilst unable to offer much positive information of their strength during successive periods, it is evident that they are decreasing in numbers.* In the country districts of the South and West of England, where Friends were formerly rather numerous, they have almost disappeared; and many of their meeting-houses or chapels, once fully attended, are now used by other religious bodies. On the other hand, their numbers have increased in many of our larger towns; thus evidencing a strong and growing disposition to follow trading pursuits in which fortunes are amassed, in preference to

---

* This remark applies to England alone; in America, as well as in Norway and Australia, and other places, they are increasing. (From information lately obtained, I find the present number of Friends is—in England about 14,000, and Ireland 3,000.)

that agricultural life, in which so many were formerly engaged. This may in part account for the fact, that whilst in 1800 the Friends had 413 meeting-houses in use, in 1851 they occupied only 371. It is probable that this general change of residence has, by unduly absorbing its members in worldly cares and money-making anxieties, materially affected both the religious and numerical status of the body.

The secession which took place at the time of the " Beacon" controversy, in 1835, (of which an interesting account may be found in the life of J. J. Gurney,) produced also a great change in many districts, more especially in the North of England. From the effects of this separation they are gradually recovering; but sufficient time has scarcely elapsed for the filling up of the gaps thus created.

It must also be borne in mind that, though the population of the United Kingdom has doubled itself within the last fifty years, the increase of church members throughout the empire is by no means commensurate with this. The fact is too painfully evident, that this augmentation of human beings swells the ranks of the irreligious world, in a much larger ratio than it does those of the church of Christ.

Although their numerical declension may therefore not be so extraordinary as would at first appear, there can be no doubt that the English Friends have neither increased, nor held their ground, in the same ratio as other denominations.

Amongst the obvious reasons for this, we may point to the large proportion of unmarried members, and to the fact that one-fifth fewer marriages take place amongst them, than is given by the average throughout the country; and furthermore, that unless both parents are actually in church membership, their children are disconnected from the Society.

It is difficult to estimate the wide-spreading effects of another law, which expels every one who marries " out of the Society," as it is termed; or, in other words, which affixes the stigma of excommunication upon any one who marries a Christian of another denomination; and not only so, but even recommends the expulsion of all "parents and guardians who may have encouraged such marriages."* The powerlessness of an indiscreet law has been strikingly evidenced by the disastrous effects attendant on its exercise. In the counties where members are most numerous, it has been ascertained that six out of seventeen of those who marry, have been obliged to leave the Society from this cause; and in country districts, where Friends are thinly scattered, the proportion is still greater.

From statistical records it appears that, during the past fifty-five years, 9,068 members have been united in marriage; and in this same period, supposing the foregoing data to be correct, no less than than 4,900 persons must have been married against the rules, and (except in very rare and peculiar cases) have been all disowned.

This harshness of expulsion from a Christian church on grounds which have no warrant in scripture, tends to alienate those who come under its operation, and there are, consequently, but very few instances of re-admission.

The only statistical accounts with which I am acquainted, give the number of Friends in England in 1800 as about 19,000, in 1840 as 16,277 persons, and in 1847 as 15,345; and from the government census of

* This law was made in the year 1752 (vide *Rules of Discipline*, p. 100). [Since this Essay was written, the marriage laws (and also the poor laws) have ben considerably modified.]

1851 it appears that at 343 chapels in the United Kingdom, on the First-day (or Sunday) morning, there were 13,361 persons present.

It must however be borne in mind that these meetings are attended by few except their own members, whilst at other dissenting chapels probably not a third of those present are actually in church membership.

The average attendance at each of the churches and chapels throughout England, according to the parliamentary census in 1851, was—

|  |  |  |
|---|---|---|
| Established Church, about | ................... | 180 |
| Baptists | ,, ................... | 130 |
| Unitarians | ,, ................... | 120 |
| Primitive Methodists | ,, ................... | 86 |
| Independents | ,, ................... | 160 |
| Wesleyans | ,, ................... | 101 |
| Brianites | ,, ................... | 72 |
| Irvingites | ,, ................... | 98 |
| Friends | ,, ................... | 39 |

(if we deduct eleven chapels of Friends, which contained more than 200 members, it leaves to each meeting-house an average of thirty).

The individual growth in grace and spiritual life which is evidenced in many of these very small gatherings, proves the extraordinary vitality of their creed under circumstances which would have extinguished the sectarian life of any other Christian sect; but it is a matter of grave importance to consider whether a religious community, under the canopy of which the soul can thus thrive notwithstanding extreme outward discouragement, is being repressed by over-legislation, or by any other needless cause, which may check the expansion from within, or turn aside the reinforcements from without. There is a warmth and a quickening influence produced by contact with large bodies of co-religionists, to which the Friends are particularly susceptible, and which is most beneficial to the growth and prosperity of every church. Were it not for the Annual Meetings in London, at which every member is permitted to attend, these scattered fragments in lonely districts would have felt in a greater degree the disadvantages of isolation from fellow-believers.

Organization and a certain numerical standing are needful for the full development of any section of the Church of Christ; without these we can have individual believers, but there can be no corporate power. It is by bodies of men acting unitedly and in harmony, that all great results in worldly affairs have been effected. However strong the head may be, it requires body and limbs to carry out its objects, and to overcome opposition. This law has ever been applicable to Christian communities, from the days when the number of apostles was increased to those in which we now live.

Another striking statistical fact is the very large proportion of hereditary members. There is no Christian sect in which so large a per-centage have inherited the tenets of their forefathers; but the deficiency of convincements far more than counterbalances any numerical advantage which is thus obtained by the retention of those brought up within the Society.

An encouraging feature may here be mentioned concerning the establishment of Sabbath-schools for the poor. In 1847 there were in the schools supported by Friends, 228 teachers and 1868 scholars; whilst in 1857 there are, in the twenty-two towns in which this work is carried on, 470 teachers engaged in instructing 3847 scholars. If the same proportionate zeal existed in all other places in which Friends reside, the number of those thus receiving tuition would be about 14,000, or larger than that of the body itself. This increased attention to supplying the spiritual necessities of the poor, has been most beneficial in its attendant results. The enlistment of the young in this self-denying work, strengthens them openly to declare their faith, and, like a Christian dress, tends to keep them from worldly associates. It also fits them for religiously instructing their own children in after-life (a power in which the Friends are often very deficient); and many who thus devote to the service of their Lord a part of those few hours which they can call their own, have been abundantly rewarded with that "blessing which maketh rich, and addeth no sorrow with it."

# CHAPTER V.

### PROGRESSIVE DEVELOPMENT.

WITH all corporate institutions it occurs that, whilst continually adding new laws and customs, they rarely cast aside any of the past. The healthfulness of all natural things consists in a perpetual addition of fresh material, and in simultaneously throwing off the old. The renewal of our bodily frame, or of vegetable and animal life, would not be possible, unless former accumulations were thus cast away the moment they become lifeless.

As time rolls on there must be a perpetual addition to the original constitution of a society; but if its members unduly venerate, and refuse to part with, those things which were life-producing only during a certain stage of existence, the framework becomes at last (like the English statute or ecclesiastical law) too formal and unwieldy for the purpose it was intended to promote.

The Friends, though radical in their general views, are extremely conservative in this respect. The obstacles raised to altering or expunging any ancient rule which the "wisdom of their ancestors" has devised, prove a stumbling-block to many who regard things on account of their intrinsic fitness and value only; and who consider more what the early Friends would have done, had they lived and preached in this nineteenth century, than what a reverential tradition for the past may demand. In observing the growth and consolidation of Quakerism, this respect for the opinions and practices of those who have gone before will be found a prominent and governing principle.*

As already expressed, the doctrines preached by George Fox were very zealously and successfully promulgated in all parts of the kingdom; persons of every rank and condition, feeling no comfort in their own priests or professions, joyfully embraced a religion which, maintaining the supremacy of Christ alone as the head of his own church, solved for them the all-important doctrine, that the soul of every man has access unto God through Jesus Christ, without the intervention of any saint, any man, any altar, or any external rite.

Having no test of membership, they included within their embrace all who came to them in sincerity; they neither established, nor allowed themselves to be called, a distinct sect, but simply came together as a society of friends. Surrounded, however, by professors of every denomination, this theory of non-organisation was found impossible in practice; and they soon had to succumb to the same laws that have governed other sections of

---

\* The Friends, in spite of their protest against human standards and authority, are very prone to contemplate the worthy deeds of their forefathers with all the reverence of hero-worship, and to rejoice in the monuments those have reared, instead of striving to raise around them other fresh tributes to the same glorious cause. The invitation to "stand in the ways, and see and ask for the old paths and walk therein," does not consist merely in recurring to the dogmas or duties of the past age, but in ascending anew, and for ourselves, to the principles of Eternal Truth, drinking at those living fountains, and from thence taking a fresh departure. It will always be easier to admire and cling to what has been, than to give new impetus to what is; but as the world is ever shifting its grounds of opposition to the church, so must the church change its attitude, and attack the predominant sins which each age produces, instead of traditionally opposing those which have either become obsolete, or been stifled by grosser and more attractive enormities.

the church. Like Luther, Wesley, Irving and others, they at first strove hard against it; but it would seem to be the sequence of every reformation, that its followers should gravitate into distinct systems.

No sooner were their views spread throughout the country, than a bitter persecution arose from all sides. The natural effect of this was to bind them yet closer together; and as in the first age of Christianity, under somewhat similar circumstances, the believers held all things in common, so did the early Friends impart freely of their substance, not alone to their fellow-professors in the same district, but, as of old, sums of money were collected, and frequently sent by well-esteemed Friends to suffering brethren in distant parts of the kingdom.

Although at an early period George Fox found it needful to institute meetings for carrying out a society discipline, such as a method of proceeding with delinquents, marriage regulations, and care for the poor and imprisoned, this was in consequence of a very peculiar position, and not an original principle. Holding the same views, Friends united together by common consent for the purpose of the public spiritual worship of Almighty God, and for the spreading of his truth ; but there was no formal admission to the rights and privileges of membership recorded by any meeting during the first century of their history.

The attendance at the conferences for the promotion of church discipline was by representation; and by appointing only zealous Friends out of the various meetings, the inconvenience of unsuitable persons taking part in church affairs did not arise. Another practical check was provided by their mode of deciding all questions propounded. During the two hundred years of their existence, no conclusion has ever been arrived at by a majority of votes, or by show of hands; Friends are encouraged freely and succinctly to express their sentiments, and afterwards the clerk records what he considers the judgment of the meeting. An admirable distinction is thus drawn between the "pillars of the church" and its smaller props; and the judgment of the veteran is not set aside by the vote of the tyro. It, however, renders the advocates of "*laisser faire*" unduly strong, and prevents any changes being made without frequent postponements, or unless a nearly unanimous feeling for change is expressed. Under the present regulations *every* individual has a voice in disciplinary meetings according to his religious stature. This alteration occurred simultaneously with the registration, as members, of all children born of Friends, and with the establishment of temporal advantages and rights in connection with it. Injurious and unlooked-for effects have followed these changes. They have caused the distinction between members and non-members to be one of earthly parentage instead of heavenly; and the line of demarcation thus set up, has grown broader and wider, until, whilst the theoretic difference exists only in the latter being excluded from the representative meetings of the body, the real and actual division is wider than that of any other protestant sect. The non-member feels that he is unattached to, if not overlooked by, the hereditary members, and that the "consistency" which would justify his applying for admission, is of a very different character from that which is required of one born within the pale.

In tracing the progress of this Society, its history exemplifies the truth of the saying that "The blood of the martyr is the seed of the church." So long as persecution continued, earnestness and zeal were everywhere apparent; the Friends devoted their whole time to the propagation of the truth, and to the comforting of imprisoned brethren; and their willingness to sacrifice their liberty, their possessions, and even life itself for the cause of Christ, and for one another, gained them many proselytes. It is not, however, by persecution that any system can be tested; the world's smiles or the world's indifference is a far more severe ordeal to undergo; and unless it have the immutable foundation, a century of toleration will generally extinguish its career.

After the Toleration Act of William III., in 1689, and its confirmation by Queen Anne, in 1702, most of the oppressive sufferings of Friends were removed;* but at this same period a reaction set in, and a lukewarmness crept over the body. The published journals of Friends of the eighteenth century,† their annual epistles to members, and the recorded minutes of advice, all shew the low condition into which the Society fell during the middle age; but it is not clear that this decline in vitality has been continuous to this day. In connection with philanthropic exertions and Christian efforts for the benefit of the whole family of man, Friends have during the nineteenth century taken a nobler stand and a wider sphere than at any former period, and have been

---

\* See *Sewell's History of Friends*, fol. ed., p. 667, &c.

† Amongst others, the journal of John Griffith, who travelled in the ministry up and down the country from 1748 to 1768, is full of evidence to this effect. Speaking of Bristol, he says, "But very little is to be seen or felt of that plainness, pure simplicity, humility, and contempt of the world, so conspicuous in their worthy predecessors." Again, after a considerable tour through many counties, he adds: "Alas! the inordinate love of worldly enjoyments, good in themselves, covers the minds of many professors like thick clay. Many in our Society, as in others, having departed from the life, rest satisfied in a profession of religion; some also have departed from the power and the form too, neither appearing one thing nor the other." &c.

ready to unite with others in any cause in which they could conscientiously engage. This labouring in the "outer court" has increased their internal life, and powerfully disseminated their religious views; and although some few may have been led away, it has enabled hundreds of their most esteemed and consistent members to solve for us the problem of a world-wide love and work, being combined with a Quaker life and faith.

To what extent individual lifelessness has increased or lessened it would be impossible to surmise. Many who now read the lives of former devoted servants of the Lord, look sorrowfully around upon the few in this day who can compare with them, and with dismay at the prospects of the succeeding generation; whilst others, seeing in those records continual allusions to a lack of zeal and love, and judging of the life of the body, not by a few extraordinary cases, but by the general health of the whole, can see nothing in the present day which did not exist to the same or a greater extent in the past.

To check the mediæval declension, greater labours were needed; but we find the travelling ministers became fewer, increase by convincement lessened, and large secessions took place; many who remained gathered about them the reputation and noble endurance of their ancestors, whilst a certain self-satisfaction displayed itself amongst numerous prominent professors, who relied more upon outward consistency with the past, than upon the spirituality of their own day. Meetings for divine worship on the week-day mornings were neglected, and, though their profession forbad absorption in worldly amusements, very many members became immersed in worldly pursuits, to the lasting injury of the church, and of their own souls.

The usual method for restoring vitality was resorted to

as spirituality lessened, the means for holding it fast were increased; a frame-work of laws and civil organisation was constructed, but it was powerless in effecting the object desired. The body in London undertook more and more the regulation of that which had previously been left to the judgment of the district meetings;* general rules (issued under the milder term of advices,) were constantly added; the number of queries respecting the external conduct of members was doubled; more and more stress was laid upon outward conformity, and those whose exterior was most consistent obtained thereby an undue sway.

Friends in the country looked increasingly for precedents and laws by which to decide those cases that had heretofore been adjudicated upon their own merits. Such centralising of the discipline had simultaneously the effect of lessening private judgment, and of raising up a church conscience, which might be universally appealed to as the standard of right order.

This infringement weakened local meetings, by an unwise removal of their responsibilities, and made them dry administrators of written laws, instead of living judges of each individual case. A comparison of the three editions of their "Book of Extracts," will shew

* To illustrate this, I may mention the subject of grave-stones. For the first seventy years Friends were allowed to exercise their own judgment, and many simple head-stones were erected during that period. In 1717, the Annual Meeting issued a paragraph, stating, "It is the advice of this meeting that they may be removed, as much as may be, with discretion and conveniency." In 1766, a stronger tone, and one which in the opinion of Friends would be considered as imperative, is adopted : " We earnestly recommend that the removal of them may become general." In 1850, although sanction is obtained for their adoption if desired, yet the Yearly Meeting, not having confidence in its subordinate meetings, undertakes to regulate not only what may be written upon them, but the position in which alone they may be placed.

the great multiplication of rules, and the very few which have been superseded or erased.* The exalting of a central church government has not been beneficial in its effects, and has evidenced that there is extreme danger, even to a society without form or ritual, of loving the frame-work and scaffoldings for their own sake, in preference to adhering to that individual conviction which was so bravely advocated by George Fox.

Of late years there has been a reactive feeling upon this system, and an increased disposition is apparent to lay upon the shoulders of right-minded members throughout the country, that share of the burden which is profitable for themselves, as well as helpful to the church; and to make each feel that he has a duty to perform to his fellow-professors, beyond that of merely interpreting laws, or seeing them rigidly enforced.

* The "Rules of Discipline" book, printed in 1783, contains 180 quarto pages, whilst that of 1852 contains 450 pages of same size.

## CHAPTER VI.

#### IMPEDIMENTS—ESSENTIAL.

HAVING passed in review the fundamental doctrines and special testimonies which the Society of Friends has ever upheld, we will now look at those obstructions to the rapid spread and reception of its tenets, which are inherent and necessarily inseparable from the principles themselves.

"The friendship of the world is enmity with God," (James iv. 4); and it must ever be, that a sect requiring, with an open confession of Christ, a perpetual self-denial and an avoidance of lawful pleasures, if they lead others astray, and the renouncing of every worldly honour or emolument which would interfere with the health of the soul, will have fewer followers than any which is less strict in its personal requirings. It is probable also, that the Society of Friends would number less than others, because it can offer no worldly inducement, neither can it attract the thoughtless or indifferent, by appealing to their outward senses and emotions. Quakerism, like Puritanism, must always remain an undesirable arena for those who are primarily attached to the fashionable world, and careless about religion.

Another large class who would be unlikely to look for consolation within its borders, are those who not only feel incapable of travelling the heavenward journey without human supports upon which to lean, and upon whose counsel they can unhesitatingly rely; but who have always looked upon the stimulants of outward ordinances, music, singing, and eloquent sermons, as necessary food for the Christian believer. The only way of disproving these ideas is by shewing living examples wherein the weakest and frailest amongst the Friends do evidently grow in grace, by looking to the Lord alone for help. It is impossible, logically, to convince a lame man that he could do without his stick, or the temperate that he would be better without stimulants. Each must make the experiment for himself, and be encouraged so to do by witnessing the effects on others. The apparent absence of any clearly recognized human counsellors for the bereaved and afflicted of soul, has often appeared an insurmountable objection to many whose life and education have been on an entirely different system. By those, however, who cease to regard religious stimulants as absolute necessaries of life, the Society of Friends has been found to contain an unusual brotherly interest and sympathy as between all its members, although it has none so exalted above the rest who can interfere with or assist in the communion of the soul with its Maker.

There are also other special hindrances to the universal spread of Quakerism, which operate to a small extent only in other denominations. For instance, the ordinary occupations for sons of the gentry are—physic, law, divinity, army and navy, and government appointments. Of these five professions, the first alone is entirely open to a Friend.

1stly.—Although he may become a solicitor or conveyancer, yet since, as a Christian, he could not advocate a cause which he knew and felt to be wrong, or make use of any argument in debate which he believed to be false, a conscientious Friend could not become a pleading counsel; and it is from out of these that the higher judicial offices are mainly supplied.

2ndly.—Preaching cannot be converted by any Friend either into a source of emolument, or a means of obtaining a livelihood, or of acquiring worldly position.

3rdly.—The profession of war, naval or military, he cannot follow, because it implies the deliberate destruction of his fellow men; and most of the government appointments being closely connected with bearing arms, there are few of such into which he could freely enter. None of their members could, with propriety, become connected with the stage or theatrical life; and their objections to music combined with dancing would prevent any amongst them from following these as a profession. Of late years only has it been considered by them that the intensely ideal life of a sculptor, poet, or painter, is compatible with the primary claims of a religious life; or that (even if lawful) such soul-absorbing pursuits can be profitable for a Christian to follow.

Whilst, therefore, the scruples of Friends against most of the fashionable pleasures of life forbid their taking part in them, the same conscientious difficulties close up to them many of its most profitable and fashionable avocations. How far these circumstances have induced their numerical decline it would be difficult to say, but they do unquestionably exercise a great influence; firstly in keeping the upper classes from joining, and secondly, in enticing wealthy members away from them.

A sound education, business diligence, and provident habits, enable many Friends to amass fortunes; and it is a natural sequence that they who inherit such will seek an enlarged field for expenditure and worldly honour. Unless occupied in philanthropic or religious affairs, a rich Friend has but little employment either in purse or pursuit; and the barrier which this religious profession offers to mixing in the 'best county society,' is a sore drawback to many an aspiring heir!

Let it not be said that such scruples render the universal spread of Quakerism impossible. If the views themselves are in accordance with the New Testament, they will prevail just in proportion as Christianity itself prevails in the hearts of its professors. How far society would thrive without counsellors who must plead on either side, or without armies who must fight as their rulers command them—how far theology could exist apart from its emoluments, or whether fashionable life, worldly honours, dancing, and theatrical pursuits, are profitable for the Christian disciple, are subjects too wide to be here touched upon; neither could any arguments, pro or con, affect the main proposition—that whatever the New Testament commands must be obeyed by all those who believe in its divine authority.

# CHAPTER VII.

#### IMPEDIMENTS—SUPERFICIAL.

### Part 1. *Misimpressions.*

THERE is unquestionably a very indistinct idea amongst the religious world upon what constitutes a real Friend. To those who do not come into personal intimacy with them, they appear a singular people, who, having originally struggled hard for individual convictions and rights, are now forgetting their mission, and, in striving after an orthodox formalism, are exalting the conscience of the sect above that of the person.

Having no initiatory ordinance, and being very diffident in discussing their principles, or explaining them; ignoring the sanctity of all material things, (such as church, chapel, altar or cemetery); acknowledging neither outward baptism nor outward supper; objecting to closing their shops on the anniversaries of those events in the life of Christ which are of vital interest to themselves, and to all Christians; refusing to acknowledge days of national humiliation, fasting, or thanksgiving, when ordered by the Queen as head of the church; and being the only Protestant sect which objects to the reading of the Bible in its public assemblies;—it is no wonder that, notwithstanding their repeated explanations, they should be regarded suspiciously, and find it difficult to convince strangers of their gospel foundation. They negative so many of the traditional notions and practices of other sects, that the *primâ facie* evidence to the casual observer is, that the Scriptures are not literally binding upon them, but that they are a highly moral, rather than a highly Christian, community.

The uniformity of their costumes, and their peculiarities of speech and manner; their extreme sensitiveness respecting their corporate reputation; the difficulty of admission into membership, and the summary way in which delinquents, both civil and moral, have been expelled, and the distinct laws by which they are governed, all confirm the impression that they are a religious order desiring less the extension of their own borders than the maintenance of a distinctive aspect.

Neither is this popular impression unfounded. From the day the Society of Friends became a civil community, as well as a religious one, there has been a constant tendency to materialize its laws. The divine principle of a church needed no human legislation; but (as in the days of the Apostles), the poor and imprisoned and suffering required outward care. From these necessities have arisen laws respecting property, insolvency, the settlement of poor, marriages, births and deaths, rules for arbitration, and numerous other civil regulations. So much, indeed, is this the case, that were the whole of their community now to emigrate in a body, they would require few additional laws of government.

It is on account of these civil advantages, and not because Friends wish to keep non-members from partaking of their spiritual privileges, that the modern exclusiveness has arisen; an exclusiveness which can only be removed by the entire readjustment of the respective claims of flesh and spirit.

There has of late been very little endeavour to gain proselytes, and their rules upon this important question are all founded on the text, "Lay hands suddenly on no man." Out of 450 pages of counsels and rules, two pages only are devoted to the subject of convincement, and no clause has been added thereto since 1807. So entirely has the number of converts dwindled away, that for a stranger in the middle rank of life to become convinced, and apply for membership, is in many districts a rare and unexpected circumstance.

By their consistent and self-denying life the early Friends established a high reputation as a moral and conscientious sect; but it is self-evident that no "name to live" could keep even its most orthodox followers from sin, or from denying the Lord who bought them.

It is not man that exalts the truth, but the truth that exalts the man, so long as he clings to it. If he relax his hold he must inevitably fall, and the higher he had risen upon its pinions, the more severe and startling will be the downfall; but to maintain that such a catastrophe proves either that he had never laid hold of the truth at all, or that if earnestly and prayerfully clung to it could not have supported him through every temptation, is grossly fallacious. The shame must always (as with Peter formerly) lie upon the transgressor himself, and not upon the faith which he forsook.

By disregarding this fact, an over-sensitiveness—I might almost say a Pharisaic pride—respecting their "corporate reputation" has crept in, and they have become not only too precipitate in repelling every attack upon their moral standing, but have too hastily repudiated the wrong-doings of those who have brought discredit upon the body. In many cases a harsh legislation and unchristian severity has evidenced a greater anxiety for the respectability of the Society before the world, than for the good of the individual transgressing.

It may be argued that the cutting off of unsound limbs tends to the preservation of the tree; but a gentle and judicious care over failing and fruitless branches may restore such to life again, and, in the end, add to the magnitude and healthfulness of the tree itself.

Whilst it is manifestly unjust to measure any sect by the frailties of professors, many of whom have never opened their hearts at all to receive the ingrafted word, I admit that, concerning its living members, " By their fruits shall ye know them." It is this absence of fruit that gives rise to the opinion entertained by orthodox Friends, that the decline of the Society is caused mainly by a lack, more especially amongst the younger, of religious individual life; and that a faithful walking of each one before God is the only means for restoring their church, and of inducing others to join them. We know that men must reach the kingdom of Heaven as individuals, and not as corporations; and that if the separate stones of a building are defective, or out of place, the symmetry of the whole structure will be marred. We know, also, that without personal faithfulness no true growth can be experienced, and that the decline or extinction of a sect ever must depend upon the decline of spiritual life amongst its individual members. But these truths only push us backwards one step farther to inquire—How is it that unfaithfulness should be more deadening amongst the Friends? and why should not the power of God enable them to hold fast their profession in the same ratio as other sects?

I am far from stating that the life of a true and consistent Friend exercises no influence over his neighbours; but is he not generally regarded as a model to be admired, rather than as an example to be followed?

He is loved by all who know his humility and integrity of heart, but he rarely attracts converts to the faith he professes. Whether it be that his peculiarities hide his principles from the eyes of others, and that they regard his external appearance and manner as the foundation, instead of the coping-stone, to his profession, may be disputed; but the fact remains, that by the serious and self-denying of other sects he is looked upon as a member of a religious order or fraternity, who is not anxious to induce them to enlist under the same banner, on their road to the celestial city.

So long as the modern Friends superadd to their pure spiritual views, a necessary external uniformity (which was no part of original Quakerism) as the gate through which converts should enter, they will be regarded as upholding a system adapted to the few, but can never become what Fox and his cotemporaries intended they should be—viz., a religious community with open doors gathering in the pious of every denomination, and with principles adapted to men of every name and nation, and of every rank and capacity.

It avails nothing that the strict and orthodox disciplinarian should content himself with the idea that Friends are more enlightened than others in their religious views. The very confession of this belief renders his condemnation the greater, if he do not strive, in season and out of season, to impart its excellencies, and in his Master's name compel the lame and the blind to come in. No degeneracy of its younger members is so paralyzing to a church as apathy in this respect amongst its elders. Although there be salvation under every Christian name, yet any individual knowing that he has found that upon which his own soul can feast, is bound by love to God and love to man to invite others to the same banqueting-house. This indifference has been most strikingly evident in many "pillars of the church," and has operated very disastrously on the minds of younger members. It encourages the notion that the duty of Friends is "to leaven other bodies," instead of increasing their own; but unless they admit that their vocation is and was as a religious order, and not as the "church of the Gentiles," no satisfaction at a small portion of their principles being embraced, should compensate for their pain that many of what they regard as most valuable testimonies are still unrecognized or rejected by others.

To be content with a partial inoculation, when they declare their mission to be the re-establishment of simple Christianity,—Christianity without diminution, and without addition,—is denying in practice what they uphold in theory, and is utterly opposed to the labours, sufferings and hardships, which George Fox and the early Friends endured for endeavouring to *spread* the truth. Had these noble-hearted men been content with having found the hidden treasure for themselves, their path would have been smooth and unmolested; but because they would never rest, night or day, without trying to bring others into the same blessed experience, they were persecuted and imprisoned to the death.

If Quakerism be not really adapted to the spiritual wants of all, then George Fox was under a delusion in promulgating a faith which was not "simple Christianity," but one suited only to a certain class; but if, as there is abundant evidence to prove, from the past histories of thousands, and from living evidences now around us, it does meet the wants of the humblest and least educated, as well as of the learned, the wealthy, and the profound thinker; no abstract ideas upon toleration, or the universality of grace, can remove the weight of responsibility which rests upon every strict Friend, to invite all men to share his special privileges.

No statement of mine can exaggerate the change in practice between the first Friends and their representatives of the present day. In the early life of the Society every member was engaged, either publicly or privately, in teaching the truth to those without the pale; hundreds of converts, from amongst the dissolute and the good, were annually made; but the impression is now so engraven upon the minds of its staunchest and strictest supporters, that the main work to do is to hedge in those who are already members, and to keep themselves a separate as well as a peculiar people; that no alarm from the watch-towers has yet been sounded, sufficient to shake that civil compact of worldly advantage which narrows the entrance to their community. My conviction is, that this entire change in the object of Quakerism is a principal cause of its decline. Laws framed upon a desire to keep up something of a Jewish theocracy, and an hereditary and distinct race, will only produce an increase of pharisaic strictness and outward profession, and members will be judged by their external consistency instead of by their sincerity of heart.

No people can become great by themselves; the help from without, exciting and adding to the energy within, is needful for the growth of every community. Unless, therefore, the Friends abandon the doctrine of fortifying their own citadel by the erection of bulwarks, fences, privileges, and protection, and go back to the good old open and world-wide principles of Fox and Barclay, they will justly suffer from that greatest of all church privations, the loss of converts gathered from on every hand. They who have gone through darkest doubts, and whose belief has cost them very much, outwardly and inwardly, will ever be the staunchest and most zealous upholders of the faith; and such men can impart to hereditary professors a corporate life and energy which they can never reach by themselves alone.

With the Friends there are no worldly inducements for making proselytes. They need neither money to support their system, nor numbers to swell their importance. The sole motive must be to extend to others the same glorious liberty of the gospel. Their work is not to attack the religions of others, but to shew to all professors a loftier and closer path—not dependent upon man's assistance, and which man can neither make nor mar.

The ordinary means of promulgating religious tenets are: by preaching, by books, by personal intercourse, and by teaching.

1stly, Preaching.—The public ministers in the Society are now but few, and their work is confined more to imparting to the assembled congregations food suited to their spiritual necessities, than in giving sectarian dissertations or expositions of their special tenets.

2ndly, Books.—The controversial works published by Friends are very numerous, but they form a theological literature very little read beyond their own pale; and the tendency of all sectarian writings is to fortify respective partizans, more than to convince gainsayers.

3rdly, Conversation.—The private influence of Friends is, as we have already observed, directed more towards "leavening others" than to gathering them in; there is also amongst them a great diffidence in speaking upon or discussing sacred things. This arises, in part, from a conscientious fear of speaking unadvisedly, or of assuming a higher position than their religious experience would warrant; but it is very prejudicial to the spreading of their principles.

4thly, Teaching.—The important office of teacher,

described in Romans xii. and 1 Cor. xii., has gradually declined amongst Friends, and is now virtually extinguished. No vocal utterance is allowed in their assemblies but that of prayer and preaching, and they have no meetings for the united reading of the scriptures. In the early days of the Society the gifts of preaching and teaching were often united (as they also were in Timothy and Paul); but in many other instances the gifts of expounding scripture and of exhortation existed apart from a ministerial call.\*

The devoting our intellectual and physical talents to the service of Christ is an acknowledged duty; and, whilst other sects have erred in allowing the office of preacher to sink down into the lesser one of teacher, the Friends have unduly relied upon the former, to the almost entire exclusion of the latter. Both are clearly of divine appointment, and any church ignoring the existence of either, or confusedly mingling them together, must become dwarfed and suffer loss.

None being approved to speak in their meetings for worship, but those who believe themselves, and whom the church believes, to be rightly called to the work of the ministry, there is no possibility for exhortation or teaching, except on private occasions, or at their disciplinary meetings, at which but few attend of those most needing instruction. "Exhorting elders," who formerly gave valuable counsel to their younger and less advanced brethren, have become fewer and fewer. There is ample

---

\* The difference between preaching and teaching is a very important one. The former is regarded by Friends as a special mission to special congregations; and the latter is the imparting to the ignorant around us those *general* truths which, in the providence of God, we have been permitted to lay hold of. The fact that, under the gospel, women are allowed to preach, but not to teach (vide note, p. 26), also shews the fundamental distinction that exists.

material within the Society out of which rightly qualified teachers could be gathered, if opportunity were afforded for such appointments. The number of ministers of the male sex has greatly decreased; yet there can be no doubt but that many teachers who thus dedicated their intellectual talents to the Lord, and faithfully discharged the lesser service, would be called, from time to time, to exercise the loftier gift of preaching.

The re-establishing of teachers would also tend to remove some of the dread and awfulness with which the ministry is regarded amongst Friends. Many to whom the truth is dear above every earthly thing, have been unduly kept back by an impression, that inspiration in its highest form is a needful prelude, and grey hairs have overtaken them before their lips have been opened publicly to declare the goodness of the Lord. Far be it from me to advocate an unauthorized ministry; but an exposition, in modern language, of the nature of that impression which rests upon the soul, when ministerial service is required of it, would check the growing scepticism of younger members concerning what is called "an inspired ministry," and would shew to them how, when a certain service is required of an individual, he may and often does intermix with it his own human feelings. These labours must be measured, not by the preacher's own ideas of its authoritativeness, but by the effects on his hearers; or, in the admirable terms of counsel (*Book of Extracts*, clause 9, p. 168): "Let none lay too great stress on the authority of their ministry by too positively asserting a divine motion :—the baptizing power of the Spirit of Truth accompanying the words, being the true evidence."

## Part 2. *Language and Dress.*

*Language.*—The objections advanced by the early Friends to the use of the plural number in addressing single individuals were,—that it had its origin in pride—that it was not the language of the Scriptures—and that it was ungrammatical.

The latter argument may quickly be disposed of, and is to be regretted that Friends should have made it so prominent. It cannot be the duty of any religious body to undertake to rectify the laws of grammar or syntax, more especially when its members are not of a learned class, or deeply versed in philology; and the universally incorrect grammar spoken by the Friends themselves,\* renders them an undesirable tribunal to express a judgment. This technical objection to a form of speech can in itself have no more connection with a conscientious testimony, than would a protest against the misuse of the relative pronouns, or the placing the nominative case after a verb or preposition. One of the greatest masters of our language regards the singular number as being,

---

\* This may be thought too sweeping a censure upon a well educated people; but whilst the middle classes in England do generally make the verb agree with its nominative case, I have never met with a Friend who in conversation did not break this first law of Lindley Murray. Thou ought*est*, thou might*est*, thou go*est*, &c., are too formal and stilted for ordinary speech, although they may appropriately be used for solemn or poetical strains, histrionic addresses, or as terms of endearment. The same cause which converted these two-syllabled verbs into one, viz., that it is less formal, more easy to pronounce, and more euphonious, led, I believe, to the ready adoption of the plural pronoun by all classes; and has also produced the ungrammatical "thee" instead of "thou" amongst Friends in the south of England. Spoken language has an invariable tendency to soften down its aspirate or rugged sounds. The past participle *ed* as in lov*ed*, is now rarely uttered except in poetry, or religious reading. A *vivâ voce* reading of Chaucer, or other early English poet, will exemplify the great extent to which these and other obstructions to a smooth diction have been removed.

from its grandeur, fitted especially for prophecy, and for addresses to the Deity, but not for ordinary parlance;* and in accordance with this view modern grammarians give the second person singular as "thou or you."

In the Holy Scriptures the singular number is invariably adopted. It must, however, be acknowledged by all, that though our translation may give the correct rendering of these Hebrew and Greek forms of expression, Biblical peculiarities are not binding in perpetuity upon any language.

We will now turn to that which formed the real objection in the mind of George Fox, viz., the pride in which it originated, and to which it pandered. In his day it was the custom throughout England (as it still is in some parts of the northern counties), to use the term "thou" in addressing equals. Believing that in the sight of God there was no distinction of persons, Fox declined using a different mode of speaking to any man, whatever his worldly position. The wealthy, regarding this departure from ordinary custom as an intentional insult, and indicative of contempt for their authority and standing, were extremely incensed thereat, and blows, abuse, and imprisonment, were freely administered to the indomitable Friends. This angry opposition confirmed the latter in the supposition that pride was at the bottom of the custom, and this "plain language" was adopted, therefore, as a direct rebuke to haughtiness.

It is however, reasoned by many, that since then, language has undergone great changes; that the singular number in the present day is never used towards equals and inferiors as it then was; that the term "you" is not intended as flattery by the speaker, nor is it so considered by the person addressed. The only objection,

* Dean Trench, on the study of words.

therefore, to its use, must be, that although not now laudatory, yet it once was so, and ought consequently to be avoided ever afterwards. To this it is replied, that external sounds are nothing in themselves; the question is, what is their meaning and intent? It would be as reasonable to object to living in a castle, or to using a Roman road, because they had their origin in evil, as to refuse to adopt a custom which once was wrong, but which in the progress of ages has parted with its impurities, and to the millions of this country conveys no idea either of pride or compliment.

The giving of flattering titles may all be measured by a like rule. If Paul applies the term "most noble" to Festus, we are justified in giving to each his usual worldly titles, if they be not false in word, or unsuited to humanity.

I cannot see how, upon the principles of Friends, that which is not evil in design, nor evil in its effects, can be inherently wrong; nor that the title Mrs. to a married, and Miss to an unmarried woman, Mr. to a man, or Master to a lad, can be sinful, when applied, as they now usually are, to both rich and poor. Without these terms our language would be defective in its descriptive power.

On the subject of days and months, the Friends are wrong in their way of carrying out a true principle.—They refused to adopt the ordinary mode, because—first, the scriptures had the simple words, first, second, &c., (although Moses speaks of the month Abib, and others, as Zif and Adar, are elsewhere alluded to);—and secondly, because they commemorated the names of heathen deities.

It is true, that the Jews were repeatedly ordered to abstain from everything that could tempt them to idolatry; and Moses commanded Israel to "make no mention of the name of other gods, neither let it be heard out of thy mouth." So great was this tendency to heathenism before the Christian era, that the Israelites, while under Mount Sinai itself, made the idol of a golden calf. The Almighty was then known only by his works, and the abstract worship of the invisible and impersonal seemed almost impossible, even with the accessories and splendour of Judaism; but since the Son of God "has been made manifest in the flesh," our shadowy conceptions of the Eternal mind are able to condense around One whom we may think of clearly as the invisible and spiritual God, revealed personally to man—"whom human eyes have seen, and human hands have handled—who loved us with a human heart—who spoke our human speech"—who, as the living Word, "was made flesh and dwelt among us" (John i. 14). This revelation in material form has destroyed that tendency to polytheism which had previously prevailed; and rarely, if ever, has a Christian nation gone back to paganism.

The two dispensations being in this respect so different, there probably could not be found any Friend who deliberately believes that the slightest temptation towards worshipping the wooden gods of our ancestors is induced by their names being recorded in our language. This fear of idolatry—the *cause* of the command to the Jews—being removed, the command itself is not applicable to or binding upon us in this day.

If this argument be not a valid one, it may further be observed that six out of the twelve months to which the Friends object are not named after gods of any kind; and their designations are adopted by nearly every civilized nation on the face of the globe.—To attempt to alter these six must evidently be beyond the functions of a religious sect.

A similar scruple would also appertain to the pagan names Pleiades and Orion mentioned in scripture—to those of the planets, Jupiter, Neptune, &c.—and to the use of words such as jovial, saturnine, cereal, mercury, martial, and many others, with their compounds; since they are equally derived from the fictitious attributes of false idols.

Language has been designated as fossil history; and in no way is this more strikingly illustrated than upon this subject of months and days. It witnesses not only that our progenitors worshipped "gods which are no gods," but that they apportioned days for the especial honour of each. We also find, from the same enduring testimony, that whilst most of the ancients united in honouring the host of heaven, and had their "dies solis" and "dies lunæ;" the other days of the week were named after their respective national gods of whom they had man-made images. Our ancestors thought more highly of their Thor and Woden than of the Roman "dies Mercurii," or the "Mardi" of Gaul.

This subject would allow a much deeper investigation; but sufficient has been expressed to show that we have thus an imperishable record of the idolatry of our forefathers. The annihilation of these Saxon words, which are the existing proof of this fact, would be similar to re-burying the Nineveh remains, or destroying the relics of Druidical worship at Stonehenge. We know, also, that the Jews were constantly commanded to destroy idols and all heathen relics; but that law is not felt to be binding upon us when we preserve Hindoo and South Sea images of gods. The temptation to idolatry must however be greater in possessing such visible embodiments, than in the mere engraving of their names upon the enduring tablet of language.

Although the dictates of a tender and scrupulous conscience produced these peculiarities in the first Friends,* I submit that since then, two centuries having obliterated the second person singular from our spoken tongue, it is not a religious duty for us to revive it either towards rich or poor; and that the honour of God is not infringed by the continuance of heathen words or their compounds in our language. They exist, not in deference to the idols, but as humiliating records of the darkness, of our ancestors.

There are many sincere-hearted Friends who conscientiously believe in these practices, apart from the illogical reasons adduced by the Society for their maintenance. With such individual scruples I have no wish to interfere;—but justice demands from them the same charitable forbearance towards those who conscientiously think otherwise.—" Let not him that eateth despise him that eateth not; and let not him which eateth not judge him that eateth: for God hath received him." (Rom. xiv. 3.)

*Dress.*—The testimony of Friends against vain customs and the spirit of the world, in apparel, furniture, or mode of living, was, as we have seen, based upon the conviction that the cross of Christ must be in all things borne.

* In connection with this subject it is somewhat remarkable, that, though the serious-minded who leave the Society generally carry with them some of its views, they have never upheld that of language; neither has a similar conviction overtaken the religious of any other sect. If the singular number were not adopted as a matter of conscience, it would no doubt still exist amongst the Friends as an affectionate form of speech, similar to that in use amongst the French and Germans.

*Simplicity* in dress was insisted on, but for the first fifty years a distinctive Quaker costume was never recommended. In progress of time the idea arose, that, as fashions were ever changing, a young man should not adopt a garb such as was worn by the serious people of his own time, but one which was usual in the days of his grandfather or father.

The early Friends adopted the costume of their own age alone, and we have no record that any of them thought the latter course to be required. They wisely refused to follow the absurdities and caprice of the empty-souled mortals who made dress the great object of existence, and declared that they should adhere through life to the attire which they found in vogue as young men, changing only for convenience sake. If the Friends had existed for 1200 years, instead of 200, and had upheld the modern theory which has crept in, of dressing like their ancestors, the effect would now be very striking. Each generation possesses a simplicity, as well as a fashion, of its own, but the term is necessarily a vague one. To the African or Malay, English clothes must appear complex in the extreme.

Had first principles been clung to, the sectarian distinction which now exists would not have arisen. George Fox held that the followers of Christ should be distinguishable from the world around them, but not that a Christian of one sect should be recognized by his attire from a Christian of another. If it be sound that a Friend should be known by his external appearance, it will apply equally to other denominations; and Baptist, Episcopalian, Independent, and all others, should be known by their respective exteriors. As professors of the same vital truths, would not their united protest against vanity do more for religion than sectarian badges could possibly effect?

I am sensible of the great advantages which the Friends' dress confers upon members. It enables them to recognize each other at all times—through it, the stranger often is invited to partake of the hospitality and kindness of unknown brethren—it is an ever available passport, if not proof, of his respectability, and very much social happiness is interwoven with this external mark of membership. Moreover, it may form a barrier from sinful amusements, and from gay and wicked associates. From its opposition to "the lust of the flesh, the lust of the eye, and the pride of life," it also acts as a self-imposed mortification upon the mind of the wearer, and is at all events less objectionable than any bodily or secret penance that could be imposed.

It is painful to probe any practice the benefits of which are so great and indisputable, and if its only disadvantages were that it makes Quakerism a hard profession, and that it encourages a pharisaic regard for the outward, I could be satisfied in passing over this time-honoured custom. If none but those who are inwardly convinced of its propriety were asked or permitted to adopt a Friend's dress, or if the form was not allowed to precede the scruple, but made to follow it, the resulting evils would be less.* But although many humble fol-

---

* John Griffith, in 1761, speaking of Pontefract Monthly Meeting, says:—" Here was a very numerous body of Friends whose outward appearance was very becoming our self-denying profession; and I really believe this plainness in a considerable number amongst them was the genuine product of a well regulated mind; yet, I fear, in too many it was more the effect of education, which, however, I would not condemn where people are not prevailed upon by the subtleties of Satan to take their rest therein; since the form must follow the power, and not the power follow the form."—(*Journal*, p. 326.)

lowers of Christ have felt, and ever will feel, called upon by a plain apparel outwardly to evidence their faith—although religious orders of monks, nuns, priests, clergymen, and pastors, adopt special costumes to show their particular fraternities, it cannot be but that the imposing on any member, or upon one who wishes to be so, an outward development for which he has no individual conviction, is subversive of ancient Quakerism.

An inward sense of what is right must precede the open profession of it; but the upholding of these scruples on dress and language, by those who cannot plead a real *conscientious* justification for so doing, is untruthful, and assuming a false attitude before the world; it beclouds the religious sense, and scepticism as to whether conscience dictates anything beyond mere educational beliefs, has not unfrequently resulted.

Friends professedly desire to embrace every lover of the Saviour, and to admit all within their fold; but their distinctive peculiarities have a direct effect in keeping them an exclusive order, and are very adverse to the general spread of their tenets.

Moreover when the young are called inconsistent, because they do not adopt the costume of a former century, and are on this account thought irreligious or careless by their stricter brethren, it creates a gulf between those who think much and those who think little of sectarian garb, which is damaging to the humility of both sections.

The world looking on, and seeing nothing in Christianity which requires antiquated garments, or obsolete terms of speech, refuses to investigate the real principles of Friends, but regards these scruples as arising out of a narrow education, and its members as rigid formalists, who pertinaciously cling to the lifeless relics of a bygone age.

These scruples cannot be tested by the law of expediency, nor by the benefits accruing to individuals who are faithful to this or to any other supposed duty. But looking at the results—the formality it leads to—the false distinction it draws between members—the loving the form for its own sake—the *primâ facie* hindrance which it offers to the universal spread of Quaker principles—and, lastly, to the fair assumption, that if the Society of Friends were just arising, and George Fox now engaged in promulgating his doctrines, he would neither adopt the plain language nor an upright collar, I do not hesitate to place amongst the main secondary causes of the decline of the Society the corporate maintenance of these two usages; involving as it must do the false principle, of many sincerely attached members outwardly professing scruples because the church thinks them to be right, but which they do not themselves inwardly feel.

The subject of Christian deportment need not long detain us. The uncovering of the head to a building or church, was an acknowledgment of the holiness of matter, and clearly inconsistent with the Gospel.

The refusal to stand bareheaded before those in authority was construed as intentional disrespect, and therefore, contrary to the command: "Honour all men, fear God, honour the king." A hat is a covering for out-of-door use; but if the postulate of Friends be admitted, that the act of taking it off *is* "an homage due to God only," the solution of this question would be easy. The sinfulness of such ceremonies must, however, depend entirely upon the impelling motive—whether as an act of worship of man, or as "honour to whom honour is due."

The apostolic declaration that "There is nothing

unclean of itself, but to him that esteemeth anything to be unclean, to him it is unclean;" and "He that in these things serveth Christ is acceptable to God;" is the true basis of conduct. If the Friends would return to their ancient doctrine, " I do it because I feel it to be right;" and cast aside the false dogma, " I do it because the Society says I ought to;" all other things would assume their proper places.

## Part III.—*Deficiencies.*

The want of corporate action whereby the early efforts of the young may be enlisted in philanthropic undertakings, and of a systematic visiting of the poor and afflicted, is much felt, and has induced many to unite themselves with other communities in which their slight services are appreciated and encouraged, and which afford in their view greater scope for usefulness.

The education of Friends admirably fits them for entering into the wants and woes of those around them. Their reputation for charity and disinterestedness is such, that the houses of the poor would be rarely shut to them; more correct impressions would thus be conveyed of their scriptural foundation; many would be induced to examine for themselves the value of the religion which their visitors practically displayed; and upon the minds of those so employed in visiting, the blessed fruits of early dedication would be evidenced. Their present casual care for the poor would be greatly advantaged by regularly organized efforts for tract distribution, clothing and sick funds, First-day schools, needlewomen's societies, and many others. The employment of all the younger members in such active engagements under the direction of the church itself would greatly cement their attachment to it, and give them an interest in all its other concerns.

The absence of all meetings authorized and promoted by the body, at which the Holy Scriptures are publicly read or expounded, has (as already stated) materially affected its increase from without and from within. R. Barclay (*Apology*, prop. 3, s. 6,) declares that "they (the Scriptures) are the only fit outward judge of controversies amongst Christians;" and, furthermore, "that the use of them is very comfortable and necessary to the church of Christ."

Now that which is "necessary for the church" should be provided by the church, and not left to individuals. Probably the Bible is more read in private amongst the families of Friends, than in any other sect; but this does not meet the circumstances of those who are unwilling or unable to read, who are invited to attend their religious meetings, and thus lose their only opportunity of hearing elsewhere the contents of the sacred volume. I am far from suggesting that the Christian duty of public reading should interfere with the still higher one of spiritual and silent worship of Almighty God, but stated times might be appointed for each service.

Very few of those who have small means of acquiring knowledge, and feel some instruction necessary, will make trial of a place of worship in which the Bible is neither read nor expounded. Again: although most Friends are well versed in the Scriptures, this cannot be said of all, whether adults or children. As regards the latter class, their Yearly Meeting of 1857 states, in its "Address to Parents," "Children continue to enter our schools very imperfectly instructed in their moral and religious duties, and lamentably ignorant of the contents of the sacred volume." It is one thing to recommend the practice, and another to carry it out—the latter can only be accomplished with certainty by the church undertaking it publicly, as well as recommending it privately. If all such readings or expositions preceded divine worship, the dull mind might ponder over truths which it had heard, even if it were too listless and indifferent to excite itself to love and praise. The outpouring of the Holy Spirit upon these occasions might be the means of awakening some to a sense of their lost condition, and others to the great reality of the soul holding silent communion with its Maker. Neither would this course be opposed to the real principles (although it is contrary to the practice) of Friends. The violent opposition which George Fox received from all sects, evidenced such an irreligious spirit and bitter fruits, that he condemned all their practices *en masse*, as lifeless and unprofitable; but this does not exonerate the Friends of later days from seeing what sound and scriptural practices in other churches might be advantageously interwoven with their own.

It is not to be presumed that Fox, or any other man, could provide for the wants of all future ages. His system proved sufficient for the scripture-versed members of his own time—it is for his followers of the present generation to see that whilst they maintain inviolate the fundamental doctrines of spiritual worship, the abolition of types, and the teaching of the Holy Spirit, they do their part in increasing that outward knowledge which the wisest and best amongst them have so strikingly possessed, and which, until some change has been made, cannot be obtained by the poor and illiterate who desire to worship God in the assemblies of their religious society.

They having reversed the saying of Paley, "That whatever is expedient is right," by declaring that "whatsoever is right is expedient," the Friends must either assume that it is not right to read the Scriptures in public, or else confess that a fear of indirect consequences prevents their consenting to perform a right act.

It may be also that a secret undefined feeling exists hat their profession does not supply all that the poor equire; and that instead of stirring themselves to provide the outward instruction needed, they sink down into a state of indifference about bringing within their fold those illiterate ones, whom, if invited, they are bound also to instruct.

### Part 4. *Over-legislation.*

The numerical increase of the Society of Friends has been much affected by laws framed with undue severity, or with reference to civil rights and privileges.

*The penal laws of marriage* have been already discussed, and proved to operate very injuriously.

*Membership by birth* must also be placed amongst the list of unsound rules which are contrary to the fundamental tenets of the Society. Conviction of the truth of its principles, and a general consistency in carrying them out in daily life, were formerly the only basis of Church fellowship.

Until some plan is adopted for distinguishing between the convinced members and those who are merely hereditary, a great laxity of religious life will display itself in their midst. Were all the children of Friends expected, at a certain period of life, to investigate for themselves the grounds of their educational faith before becoming full members of the Church, it might not only strengthen the body by separating those who prefer remaining probationers or half members, but also induce a closer study of the lives and principles of Friends, and lead to an honest examination of many things which are now received on tradition, or on the faith of others.

Church fellowship being clearly ordained in the New Testament, entails upon every Christian the duty of attaching himself to that community in which his convictions are most nearly professed; but it was not formerly required that a convert to Quakerism should subscribe to every tenet. The applications for membership have been, and now are, materially affected by an expected conformity in non-essentials, as well as fundamentals; such requirement is not in accordance with that gradual growth unto perfection that is a distinguishing mark of the Christian's path, which "shineth more and more unto the perfect day." It is asking of the Christian tyro the same full development which has matured during long years in those who have "fought the good fight and kept the faith." The youthful David declined the armour of Saul because " he had not proved them ;" and it is injurious to press the perfect weapons of the veteran upon the unpractised shoulders of the stripling.

*Laws for the Poor.*—The principle of district collections for the support of those in destitute circumstances is admirable; and it is a fixed regulation amongst the Friends that they support and educate their own poor, and that no member ever receives parish assistance. There may perhaps be somewhat of pride in maintaining this excellent law, which is, in theory, the same as that upon which the poor-laws of this country are based,— viz., the duty of the rich to support those who are in penury. The Friends apply that care over their own religious fraternity which the State professes to do over its citizens. It does not seem more derogatory for a

Friend to receive help in part from a national fund, to which all pay, than from one raised amongst themselves; but any parish allowance would be thought a disgrace to the body at large. The great accumulation of legacies for the poor, and the thorough way in which all members are educated, prevent the charity of Friends from being unduly drawn upon; and it would not be worth mooting whether the national, the Christian, or the sectarian tie be the most fitting to supply bodily wants, if it were not for indirect results arising out of the latter theory.

The absence of a labouring class amongst the Friends is a great loss to them. None but such can fully realize the prayer, "Give us this day our daily bread;" and the living faith of the poor of this world affords practical lessons of a simple and confiding trust in God which can be ill spared by any church. The real blessings of a Christian life are most strikingly evidenced in the families of toil-worn artizans, and without a large admixture of such a Christian sect does not thrive.

The law of compulso-voluntary support of their own poor acts prejudicially in keeping such people away. It is likely to deter honest but independent spirits from applying for membership, lest they should be suspected of seeking temporal provision; and it renders Friends unduly cautious concerning the worldly prospects of those seeking admission. The expunging of this law would not lessen the private claims of fellow-believers, but it would break down the conventional civil barrier which now divides members and non-members, and open the door for free admission to all who were united with the Friends in their religious views. Until these laws are swept away, Quakerism can never become the church of the poor; for the admission of a few thousand operatives and their families would render occasional parish relief absolutely necessary.

*The rules respecting Bankruptcy* shew the indiscriminating character of the age that made them. Commercial disasters and failures frequently occur without any moral blame attaching to the individual; but disownment often succeeds, especially if it brings "discredit on the Society." If retained in membership, an insolvent continues subject to harsh and unchristian rules. The Yearly Meeting advice of 1721, that if, after a legal composition with creditors, he should at a future time be blessed with sufficient means to pay in full, it should be accomplished, is strictly right; but how different is the rule passed in the dark age of 1780, which prescribes that, unless this be done (no matter how uncontrollable the calamity, or how purifying the ordeal of temporal affliction), such person is henceforth forbidden to subscribe to the only fund of the Society which has for its object the advancement of Christ's kingdom upon earth! Although his life should be prolonged for half a century, and his self-denial be ever so great, he may contribute nothing towards the expenses of any minister travelling in the service of the gospel, nor to any of the corporate Christian efforts of the body. The elders and overseers of the present day do not hesitate to ask for, and take, his subscriptions for any private charities with which the Friends are connected; but he is not allowed to add his quota (be it ever so small) to the district fund for the corporate support of the poor. This pharisaic distinction between public and private collections cannot be justified by any law except that of cleansing the outside of the platter. These and other similar legal niceties produce an unfavourable impression upon those who are affected by them, and tend to confirm the dissatisfied in their protests against the outside profession which, since 1760, has been so prominent.

There are other obstructive laws of this period to which we might allude, all emanating from the same error which has befallen other churches; viz., that of making civil privileges and civil penalties contingent on spiritual profession. The disseverance of these two opposites would moderate that church authority in secular things, which has in many sects been converted into an instrument of oppression and wrong, and which, by its rigid exercise, has often (more especially amongst the Friends in Ireland) been very detrimental to the real interests of this community.

One great object of church discipline is to win back and restore the wanderer; but if carried out harshly, and in an intolerant spirit, it becomes, like the Romish Inquisition, an engine of persecution, hardening the hearts of those who administer, and of those who suffer from it.\* A religious body may keep itself pure by expelling all who are unruly; but the loving spirit in which faithful Friends plead with and compassionate the fallen, and mourn over the loss of every brother, is the true source of church vitality.

The non-authority of any man, or body of men, over the consciences of others, was a prominent feature of early Quakerism which the present age has too much overlooked. To threaten any member who is attached to the Society with expulsion, because he is unable to see with Friends on a minor point, or because he differs in opinion upon the way in which any testimony should

---

\* The extent to which the authority of the Church may be exercised upon its members is difficult to define. Church discipline amongst the Friends was formerly confined to things immoral or sinful, and church counsels and exhortations were directed against that which was inexpedient and liable to abuse. The legal spirit of 1760 to 1800 confused this broad line of demarcation, and inflicted dealing and disownment for acts not forbidden in Scripture or sinful in themselves.

be outwardly borne, is demanding of each person an exactness of religious development which cannot but trench upon the rights of individual conscience. Much of the present anxiety of Friends to preserve a uniformity of practice in everything, arises from an extreme desire to preserve themselves from charges of inconsistency. A "fear of what the world may say" was no part of the creed of their predecessors, and is unworthy of their own reputation; and the laying down of detailed regulations for the guidance of a people who are so professedly conscientious and independent, can never accomplish the proposed good.

# CHAPTER VIII.

### CONCLUDING REMARKS.

HAVING endeavoured, by a general examination of the doctrines and practices of Friends, to ascertain the causes of their strength as well as the causes of their weakness, a few observations seem needful in conclusion.

If I have any right apprehension of those things which are producing a decline in a religious body, which, in spite of present appearances, I believe to be destined to occupy a far higher position amongst Christian sects than it has ever yet attained, it is not the fundamental principles of the Society that have been undermining either its corporate or individual life; neither is its declension to be explained by an incorrect basis underlying any of the ancient testimonies which it has upheld.

If we for a moment direct our attention solely to the spiritual part of Quakerism, we see a faith simple and evangelical, and a life devoted and self-denying; and year by year portions of its tenets are increasingly acknowledged by other religious professors.

The main objections which have been raised against its practical application are,

1st. That it is not adapted for human wants, because mankind require outward helps and stimulus.

To this argument we reply that many thousands and

tens of thousands of Friends have proved experimentally that such are not essential to the Christian believer; but that for every mental capacity, from the simple-minded Samuel Bownas, Thomas Shillitoe, or John Upton, to the erudite Thomas Lawson, Dr. Fothergill, or Joseph John Gurney, it has been abundantly evidenced that Christianity, as professed by the Friends, not only exalts every soul, but makes a pathway in which the wise and the ignorant, the wealthy and the wayfaring man, can travel side by side, and add to each other's knowledge of divine things.*

2nd. It is contended that if Friends admitted the two ordinances of Baptism and the Lord's Supper, many more would flock to their standard.

To this it may be replied, that the secessions from the Friends upon these grounds, though very considerable, are by no means greater than upon some other points. Moreover, two centuries have proved that those who were outwardly baptized (before joining Friends) have never felt that this privilege raised them one whit above those who were not; nor that the spiritual communion with God in silent adoration was less real than that of the communion service. On the contrary—when with humble and contrited souls they have met together livingly to feed upon the body and blood of Christ, and to offer living silent praises unto Him, He hath ofttimes been in their midst, and, in the language of the prophet, " hath opened the windows of heaven and

---

* In connection with this universal adaptation of Quakerism, it is somewhat singular that the three individuals who stand out the most prominently, and are generally considered as its first representatives and exponents; viz., Fox, Penn, and Barclay; should also represent the three great divisions of society—the unlearned, the statesman, and the scholar. The poor, the highborn, and the middle class are each undesignedly typified by this, and the poorest class stands first in the category.

poured them out a blessing that there hath not been room enough to receive it."

Again: however great the loss of numbers may be in this respect, their principle absolutely forbids relaxation. So long as they read the New Testament with the preconceived impression that Christianity is in its nature and essence a religion of realities, and not of symbols— that outward washings and baptism under the law typified the cleansing of the soul by the operation of the Holy Ghost, and outward feasts and fasts the nourishment and fasting of the soul—that the costliness of burnt offerings symbolized those spiritual sacrifices acceptable unto God through Jesus Christ—and that, though our Saviour permitted his disciples to use types, He did not institute any such as binding on them or the Gentile converts—it is clear that the Friends could not conscientiously admit as essentials two opposite things—those which are typical and those which are real. Other sects, reading the Testament with the preconceived idea that two external symbols or sacraments, (or seven as the Roman Catholics maintain) were attached by our Lord to a religion that in every other particular supersedes and excludes types, do not feel any contradiction in this intermingling of shadow and substance.

3rd. The formality of Quakerism is stated to be a powerful cause of decline. Upon this head it is not needful to enlarge further.

4th. *Individual unfaithfulness.*—This term requires explanation. Does it signify my unfaithfulness to the light that is in me, or to the light that is in some one else?—to the principles of Friends, or to their practices? —to the inward or outward development of gospel truth? If the latter, I would ask whether that externalism which one class of objectors urge as the cause of decline, and which another class support, as the main source through which a revival can come, does not operate injuriously, by causing those who do not unite with it to be *ipso facto* considered unfaithful. The arguments made use of in its support are often felt by the young to be obsolete or illogical, and the education of a Friend prohibits his *blindly* following his religious superiors.

The feeling that by his elder brethren he is regarded and talked of as inconsistent, because he does not measure himself by another person's standard, is very disheartening to the weak or wavering member. It freezes within him the sense of mutual appreciation ; he cools towards the body; and the badge of worldly-mindedness, thus prematurely affixed, not unfrequently works out its own fulfilment. In other cases, where a sincere attachment to the general principles of Friends enables him to outlive this, a hearty co-operation with the body is practically excluded. It has been, until very lately, so taken for granted that every true Friend 'must think it right to adopt a sectarian dress, and a peculiar language, that those who do not have been excluded from many of the most useful offices of the Church, such as elders, overseers, clerks, and correspondents, or members of the " Meeting for Sufferings." The alternative left for one anxious to fill any post for which he may appear otherwise qualified, has been either to acquiesce outwardly, or else to forego a life of serving the cause which is most dear to him.

May it not therefore prove that "individual unfaithfulness to their principles" is not the cause, but the consequence, of a corporate decline ; and that the germ of future mischief was planted a century ago, when the orthodox Friends forsook their foundation, and, forgetting that the body without the spirit *must* be dead, tried to build up a spiritual church by an external framework?

5th. *Riches.*—The Friends being very generally a prosperous people, and not given to worldly amusements, are especially prone to disregard the injunction, " If riches increase, set not your heart upon them," and to love mammon more than God. Wealth cannot, however, be called a primary cause; since such admission would simply be an acknowledgment that Satan had made use of these secondary means to induce them to love earthly more than heavenly things. Riches are a blessing in themselves, and though our unwearied adversary very often succeeds in converting these and other outward blessings into temptations to forget God, the evil root must lie deeper. There are abundant witnesses, both living and departed, to prove that to the true and consistent Friend the increase of riches will brighten and strengthen, rather than undermine, his religion. To the nominal member of every sect, a life of ease and luxury must necessarily lessen or destroy his religious stature.

6th. *The Absence of fixed Ministers.*—Many Friends assert that this is a secondary cause produced by the deadness of the members themselves; whilst others, on the contrary, declare that spiritual deadness is the result of a lack of human ministers. There may be truth in each statement; but if admitted as a whole, the Society of Friends is doomed to decay; action and reaction will become less and less, until lifeless ministers and lifeless audiences respectively destroy each other. We do not, however, find that Paul's preaching depended on the "life" of his hearers for its exercise—his recorded labours would seem to have been principally with lukewarm audiences, and the greater their inanity the more earnest and frequent were his pleadings with them. Was it not also to the stiff-necked and uncircumcised of heart, and not to the elect and living, that Stephen preached?

If (as all acknowledge) outward ministry was ordained of Christ, it seems reasonable that the deadness of the hearers should increase, rather than diminish, the exercise of the gift. The Holy Spirit is the cause, preaching the means, and conversion the end, of all church communion; and in the divine economy each is necessary, and made instrumental to advance the other.

As already stated, the encouragement of the gifts of exhortation and teaching would bring forward many who now stand all their day idle as in the market-place, pleading the ancient excuse, "that no man hath hired them;" but who, if rightly employed in the Lord's vineyard, and having proved "faithful in a few things, would be made ruler over many things;" and, finally, be sent forth to sow "that seed, which is the word of God."—(Luke viii. 11.)

7th. It is also said that the Friends rely so entirely upon the "wisdom of their ancestors," that their profession does not adapt itself to the present age, and from this circumstance they become smaller and smaller. Having commented already upon this plea, it is not necessary to discuss it further, beyond the general remark that there is not always (as the Friends frequently reason) "safety in standing still." If the world advances and we remain stationary, our position is retrograde. Many laws and usages suited for the religious condition of the Roman and Greek in the first century, may be ill adapted to the state of English society in the seventeenth; and externals which were significant and right in the days of the Stuarts, may be meaningless or inappropriate now. Principles are unchanging, but practices are ever varying.

Other lesser objections might be named as combining to produce the declension of Quakerism, but sufficient have been alluded to in detail to account for a far worse state of things than really exists. Had there not been very much that was sterling, sound and true, in those principles which, in their original purity, induced multitudes of religious professors of every denomination to attach themselves to the despised and persecuted Quakers, the Society could not have withstood the effects of over-legislation combined with extreme conservatism, and a century and a half of State toleration.

I will therefore repeat that which appears to be the real basis of decline in this community — viz., "The departure of its orthodox supporters from the first faith and creed." Whether Friends as a body may turn again and rebuild the waste places of their city, or whether the language shall be applied to them—"They that are bidden shall not taste of my supper, for they are unworthy"—it is not for me to predict: but of one thing I can have no doubt—"*That the wedding chamber will be furnished with guests,*" and that the fundamental principles originally promulgated by George Fox and his cotemporaries, and the fundamental testimonies for which they suffered, will be upheld, even though the people themselves to whom the Lord hath given this goodly heritage, and who for many generations have received through it the choicest of earthly blessings and of heavenly joys, should be driven from out the land.

Because they have for long years not invited all around them to come and share their privileges—and, misunderstanding their corporate duty, have substituted for innate conviction, a something composed as of iron and miry clay; and have tried to amalgamate that which can never permanently unite, viz., an earthy uniformity of development, with the iron strength of inward spirituality ;—I say, because this has been done, and the land flowing with milk and honey has thus been made to appear barren, dry, and unfit for *all* the tribes of the people to dwell in, it may be in the future that lies before them, and to which my human reasoning points, that Friends will wrap yet closer around them the relics of formalism and exclusiveness as a garment, and that a people of another name. may rob them of their spiritual inheritance!

As a member of the Society of Friends by birth, and as a member by conviction—as one who owes, under Providence, all his outward blessings and most of his inward consolations to an education within its pale, and to an acquaintance with some of its living members; and ardently desirous that they who follow after should partake of the same inestimable social and religious privileges, I earnestly long—nay, it is my fervent prayer —that this may be averted. I cannot, however, close my eyes upon the crisis that is as yet far off, but which appears to be approaching; wherein, if the consistent Friends (I use the term conventionally) regard the "inconsistent," as doing violence to their own internal convictions, or else as careless about religion; and the latter look upon their stricter brethren as "taking tithe of mint, and anise, and cummin," and as judging them who to their own Master must stand or fall; if the fall of the one or the irreligious life of the other be construed as a type, instead of as an exception, to the general correctness of each class, a division into two sections may arise—mutual misunderstanding will produce mutual distrust, and each regarding the case as hopeless, unless the other becomes more enlightened, will, while thinking to do God service, be unwittingly destroying the spiritual lives of His servants. If the strictly educated Paul found that by indulging a judging spirit he mistook Satan's work for the work of God, and persecuted all who did not see with him; and if the erring Peter was still loved and tenderly regarded, until eventually he became the boldest advocate for the truth; may it not possibly result, that as between the orthodox and the unorthodox, when they learn to judge very honestly of themselves, and very charitably of all others, each may have to confess with gratitude, as well as with astonishment, in the language of the patriarch Jacob, "Behold the Lord was here, and I knew it not!"

Of you, the young members of the Society,* of whom it may be said in a truer sense than at many former periods of Quaker history, "Ye are strong, and the word of God abideth in you," I would ask earnestly, Let not the formalism nor the traditions of any man blind you to the intrinsic merits of the creed you profess; examine for yourselves, and remember also that your inner faith must in some way expand itself into an outward confession of Christ, that "He also may confess you before His Father and the holy angels." "Faith, if it have not works, is dead, being alone:" but let no laudable desire to conform to the faith and practices of others, rob you of the consolations which flow from doing that which you individually believe to be required at your hands.

To you, the elder brethren, who, having borne the burden and heat of the day, are now faint with dis-

* This and the two succeeding paragraphs were erased by the writer as unsuited for a general essay, but are now re-inserted.

couragement, because so few come up to your standard, the text may be applicable,—"Man looketh to the outward appearance, but God looketh at the heart." It was not one of the comely sons of Jesse whom Samuel anointed, but one whose existence was hardly recognized in Israel. If "the form be lifeless, unless animated by the power," it must be primarily important to cultivate the spiritual; and though in your experience the framework and outward props of the Society may have been highly beneficial, others may find more vitality without them.

Upon you, the middle-aged, will devolve the deepest responsibility in connection with the future. You who have the confidence of the aged, and the esteem of the young, may be instrumental in closing and uniting much that might otherwise produce alienation. By wise and timely concession to what is strictly sound; by the gradual removal of every abuse and formality which has crept in since the seventeenth century, and by the resuscitation of much that has crept out; by the cautious admission of needful things, and by a Christian opposition to needless ones, you may greatly consolidate and revivify the church. By assigning a right place to every member, "the eye cannot then say unto the hand, I have no need of thee; nor again the head to the feet, I have no need of you." The body is not one member, but many; and may every member be baptised by one spirit into one body, and be all "made to drink into one spirit."

I have stated that the principles of the Society of Friends must remain. If, as protestant believers, we look around upon the present aspect of Christianity,— we see Roman Catholicism pressing at every point— Jesuits engaged in every city promulgating their tenets;

the Church of England, distracted on the one hand by German rationalism, and on the other by discussions between its highest professors, upon questions which its former martyrs died in refuting; the re-establishment of the confessional—of the priestly office—baptismal regeneration—extreme unction—and prayers intoned in a manner as unintelligible to the people as ever the Latin tongue was formerly. All these things are fiercely contended for, in addition to candles, altar, genuflexions, and priestly surplices and ceremonial, resembling more the splendour of the Jewish ritual than the religion of the lowly Jesus, which was promulgated by fishermen in their simple dress. We see dissenters more and more seeking worldly honour and popular fame, to the detriment of that honour which cometh from God only. Their chapels increase in costliness and show; and their ministers, tempted by respective congregations, vie with each other in intellectual acumen and oratorical display, rather than, like Paul of old, "knowing nothing amongst them but Jesus Christ, and Him crucified;"—doing and offering with a view to popularity, that which should be performed only in humility and the fear of the Lord.

Finally, we have around us, on every hand, a huge mass of infidelity and scepticism, which will lay hold upon every flaw and every weakness in the religion of others, and out of this rotten and lifeless compound endeavour to build up a negation of faith, or a nihilism, baseless as a dream and barren as the desert; who, adopting the worst forms of Benthamite philosophy, attribute every act to a selfish motive, and refuse to believe in the constraining love of Christ leading to a purely disinterested care for the welfare of others.

Under such antagonisms, no earnest section of the one

universal church can be spared, and least of all that of the Society of Friends.

A religion in which its ministers have, neither directly nor indirectly, any worldly benefit from preaching; which seeks to gain no spiritual power over its converts; which acknowledges no human head to which all must submit their consciences; which, objecting to state patronage as much as to state persecution, tolerates the creeds and the conduct of all other sects, and rejoices so that Christ be everywhere preached; which allows the various offices of the church to be filled by persons of every rank and occupation, and measures each by his spiritual stature, and not by his classical lore or his worldly position; which desires its members to be mingling in the world, though not of it; and sees in Christianity a faith not made for any man to live at ease under, or to gratify his fleshly desires, but expects its ministers to support themselves as Paul did (Acts xx. 34, and xviii. 3), when not actually engaged in travelling on Gospel service;— a sect which upholds that glorious Scripture doctrine containing within it the highest development possible for humanity;—viz., that Jesus Christ, who hath "washed us from our sins in his own blood, and hath made us kings and priests unto God," has thereby lastingly established unto each of us the power of immediate communion with God, without the intervention of any human priest, saint, or altar.—A sect with such principles and such development is a living rebuke to all scepticism, and of no small importance to the progress of vital Christianity.

The early Friends practically carried out the duty of self-denial, and regarded all mankind as stewards of God's earthly gifts. In every philanthropic work, every generous action, they did it "not as unto men, but unto God;" not as moralists or utilitarians, but because the love of Christ constrained them." They sought not to dishonour their Lord, by taking the credit of charitable deeds to themselves; but desired to cast all their crowns at His feet, whose they were, and whom they served.

Under this feeling, the Friends are satisfied in performing a required duty, although its effects may prove fruitless. They proceed in faith, nothing doubting but that God will bless the doers of a right act, although they may fail in accomplishing the intended end.

The example of social life set by the Friends is also valuable. Their domestic comforts and rational mode of living have made them longer lived than others, and provided great happiness at a small expenditure. After no slight suffering and reproach they have shaken off the wide-spread tyranny of fashion; so much so, that " being a Friend" is sufficient excuse to the world for not adopting its customs. Their women are at liberty to follow the remains of loved ones to the grave, and they are not obliged to publish their grief to the world by mourning costume, graduated according to public opinion, and not by affection.

Their emancipation from conventional bondage preserves them from hired mutes and mourners, and from extravagant modes of interment; also from mis-spending their time or substance with reference to what others might say of them. They are sheltered from the mortifications, envy, and detractions of a ball-room existence. They prefer the love and respect of those around them, to the passing admiration of strangers. The education of their women is sound, domestic, and intellectual; neither are they deficient in any physical accomplishments, except those of instrumental music* and of

---

* Their discouragement of music seems needlessly stringent, although Plato, in his *Model Republic*, rejects all music which either inflames the

dancing; like the serious of other sects, they hold a conscientious objection to the latter.

Much more might be added to these legitimate results of Quakerism, but my object is not to extol the Society, but to glance at what it really is—religiously, morally, and socially. Its philanthropic labours are universally lauded; too much so, probably, for its own good; and require no description in these pages. The civil privileges of its members have been won through long and patient sufferings, and prove the irresistible force of passive resistance—they accomplished far more by offering up a few devoted lives in testimony of their sincerity, than the Covenanters did by the sacrifice and slaughter of thousands. Again: the execution of one woman Friend, Mary Dyer, at Boston, for the cause of religious freedom, broke down a disgraceful and anti-Christian law, which no armed force could have destroyed.

The ethics and metaphysics of Quakerism have yet to be written. Should such a task ever be undertaken, there will be found interwoven with its tenets the focus from which many philosophic systems have radiated. Its doctrines of the inward light, of conscience, of moral law and of moral force, rightly understood, would strip spiritualism of its human falsities, and materialism of its excrescences, and might reveal that one centre of

---

passions or produces effeminacy; or which, while soothing the ear, does not improve the mind. Its exclusion amongst Friends has in practice been beneficial, in inducing them to cultivate the intellectual, instead of spending immense time over sensational gratification; it has also shielded them from many temptations consequent on musical indulgence. Since, however, no gift of Providence is bestowed in vain, the Friends have yet to explain for what purpose (except a lawful exercise of its powers,) the sense of harmony, or a "fine ear," has been bestowed, throughout all ages, upon multitudes of every clime and tongue, as well as upon their own members.

F

absolute truth from which all the various and conflicting theories have diverged or gone adrift, and in which alone their distorted truths can ever harmonize.

If, both theoretically and practically, the results of this profession are such as we have sketched out, can it be said, either that its work is accomplished, or that its decay would be good for Christianity, or for humanity?

I have not intentionally added one iota to the original New Testament doctrines and testimonies upheld by the early Friends; neither does it seem needful to take aught from them, in order to account for the decline of this Society. Had it not been immutably based upon the one sure foundation, it could not have survived as it has done. Conventional hindrances have been adduced, sufficient to destroy a community far mightier than the Friends have ever been; yet, if the orthodox and the heterodox will afresh study the first principles upon which this Society was based, and cast aside all preconceived notions or traditional maxims as to what these were, it may be shewn to the former, that what they have upheld as original basis, has been, to a great extent, the innovation of the middle age; and to the latter, that the simplicity of Quakerism is, in reality, the majesty and grandeur of a divine faith.

The kindly feeling evidenced towards the Friends by those from whom they doctrinally differ is very pleasing. There is much gospel work to be accomplished, and but few labourers for the work. May every sect be found occupying its proper place in the church militant here, and their respective followers, whilst outwardly differing from one another, be lovingly united under Christ, the One great Captain of our salvation; striving diligently to advance the coming of His Kingdom, until the dawn of that glorious day, when, to all of us, "the Church and the world shall become one—where work shall be worship, and labour shall be rest—where the worker shall never quit the temple, nor the worshipper the place of work; because 'there is no temple therein, but the Lord God Almighty and the Lamb are the temple thereof.'"

# SUPPLEMENTAL CHAPTER.

Since the preceding essay was penned, in 1858, an increasing disposition has been evidenced within the Society of Friends to value things by their intrinsic importance, rather than by antiquity of origin. Conferences composed of members from all parts of the country have been summoned to consider the laws relating to marriages and to the settlement of poor, and the propriety of church dictation on matters of individual duty; and large committees have been formed to suggest alterations on questions relating to internal government.

The earnest Christian spirit evidenced on these occasions has been very encouraging; and the full discussions which have taken place have shown a religious vitality in its older and younger members, which justifies a more hopeful view of the future. Amidst great diversity of sentiment, a strong brotherly charity amongst themselves, and an increasing zeal to spread the gospel amongst others, have been displayed; and labourers from on every hand have appeared ready to obey with joyful alacrity the command to go forth once more in aggressive array against the powers of darkness.

It would be premature to offer any opinion upon the effects produced upon the Society by the published essays; and in commenting on the contents of any of them, I desire to do it, not as a critique on its merits or demerits, but in order to examine the principal arguments advanced against Quakerism as a creed. It has been well said of theological controversy, that though it may fill the head it will empty the heart; and the unimpassioned and dry manner with which an honest critic treats the most vital subjects* is injurious both to readers and writers.

The conclusions at which the second prize essayist† has arrived are in such singular antagonism to those contained in the preceding pages of this volume as to deserve careful analysis. Whilst study of the subject has convinced me that Quakerism cannot and will not fall, he has read himself into the belief that it will fall—that "its salvation is impossible," and that he rejoices that it is so. Our respective hopes and wishes may have materially affected these opposite deductions; yet it is perfectly natural that an author who holds so strongly as he does the dogmas of a "sacrificing priesthood and apostolic succession" (see p. 235), should long for, and rejoice in, the extinction of a sect whose very existence is a perpetual protest against such assumptions; nevertheless I cannot banish my own conviction that so long as there are devout Romanists or Tractarians insisting in words upon the necessity of ceremonies, and the efficacy of outward rites, so long will there be devout Quakers who by their lives will refute them.

The *unity of basis* which the author so carefully proves to exist between the writings of Dr. Pusey and the principles of Quakerism is undeniable; and I should attribute the vitality of both to their upholding those glorious truths which T. Hancock states, "though witnessed to in the liturgy of the crushed and hidden church, were

* "A *desired* result is no result. It is with the reason alone that researches must be made. A perfect disinterestedness, a supreme indifference, are the conditions of strictness. When you are sufficiently indifferent, sufficiently dry, sufficiently dead,—you are able to examine. Green wood smokes."—*Vinet's Studies on Pascal.*

† *The Peculium,* by T. Hancock.

not witnessed to in the formulas of the dominant sects; but which it pleased God to make known and heard through the preaching of the Quakers" (p. 141). These were: 1st, "That Christ doth, through the Holy Ghost whom He hath given unto us, dwell really and truly in the hearts of the faithful, and in the individual soul." 2nd, "The indwelling Spirit as the bond of church unity." 3rd, "His moving of the will as the principle of Christian conduct" (p. 235). The strong and distinct recognition of these gospel truths has doubtless given to Puseyism its expansive force. By this, rather than by the maintenance of any "sacraments, rites, and written offices," it has gained converts; and by clinging fast to these soul-satisfying truths it may continue to increase, in spite of its human errors and church traditions.

In comparing Quakerism with Puseyism, we must not, however, be content with discovering their points of union only. We acknowledge that they do converge in these three fundamental doctrines of the New Testament, and the Friends desire nothing more;—they will admit of nothing less than that the same New Testament shall become the standard for all practices and doctrines wherein they differ,—that each may renounce all that is contrary to and not contained in its divine teachings. It may be thought that by this appeal the Friends might have to add something to their *no-forms;* but none can doubt that Anglo-Catholicism would thus lose very many of its forms. It would also be seen that the former possesses those gospel realities which the latter seeks after through symbols; and by abandoning the types, and embracing the doctrinal antitypes, we should behold an English church displaying not only an apostolic zeal in spreading its principles, but an apostolic simplicity in its practices.

The way in which the New Testament is avoided as the standard of appeal is painfully evident in *The Peculium*. The whole volume is made to twine around one central column of church formulas. It is comparable to a spiral staircase, whose symmetrical proportions and carefully selected materials are in strict harmony with the shaft around which they revolve, and upon whose soundness and strength the entire framework depends. Having no power to expand beyond the radius of "church authority," it is irrevocably bound to that standard for support; but had this central column been one of New Testament doctrines, instead of church traditions, how different would the superstructure have proved!—how very different would have been his landing-place! In lieu of "a sacrificing priesthood," we should have beheld the Christian prophet and preacher; and the "*ism* of Dr. Pusey" would have disappeared under the inspired writings of the Apostles.

The High Churchman and the Friend unite also in idea that the true and apostolic church alone can permanently remain, but they differ widely upon its essential characteristics. T. Hancock asserts its form to be best upheld "when she sees most in sacraments, rites, and written offices, and when she grasps most firmly a sacrificing priesthood and apostolic succession." The Friends, on the other hand, finding none of these things ordained in those divine writings which, as Barclay declares, are "the only fit outward judge of controversy amongst Christians," believe this church to be built wholly "upon the foundation of the apostles and prophets, Jesus Christ *himself* being the chief corner-stone." "In whom (saith the Apostle) ye also are builded together, for an habitation of God through the Spirit" (Eph. ii. 20-22). No church councils or edicts can overthrow the Scripture truth that every church, wheresoever existing, and under whatever name, which is thus builded together in Christ, and which through the Spirit becomes the "habitation of God," is part of the one spiritual building—the church apostolic—the temple holy unto the Lord. It is of this universal church that it is also declared, "now ye are the body of Christ, and members in particular;" like the hand with the foot, its members must be in intimate relation to each other, and be all united with the living Head. "For we, being many, are one body in Christ, and every one members one of another" (Rom. xii. 5). This is the one true church of the apostles, and no human viaducts or hereditary channels can make or mar its essential connection with Christ, neither can any outward shibboleth represent or enclose all of its living members.

Innumerable attempts have been made to institute a visible system of church fellowship, co-extensive with this invisible bond of union; but of none can it be averred either that it included *all* who were baptized into Christ, or that it did not include many who were "dead in trespasses and sins." Romanism, by preaching regeneration through water baptism, may assert that all within its pale are of the body of Christ, and all beyond it are reprobates; but the falseness of such theory is self-evident, since it encloses thousands of unconverted and carnal men, and excludes thousands of the converted. A similar admixture in a greater or less degree exists in every church community, including both Friends and Tractarians. There are many who are dead within the fold of each, and many who are living without. Whilst it cannot, therefore, be avowed of any outward church that *all* its members are thus builded together for the habitation of God through the Spirit, the one test of membership does interpenetrate every Christian sect.

The attempt of any religious community to claim divine authority or precedence on any other grounds than the indwelling of Christ is unsound and dangerous. Every church must be apostolic if Jesus Christ himself be the chief corner-stone; and every church is unapostolic wherein His place is usurped, or wherein practices not ordained in the New Testament are insisted upon as needful or binding.

Various schemes have been adopted to bring all Protestant denominations under one outward canopy or evangelical alliance, but they produce a cessation from hostilities rather than a vital unity. The simple apostolic foundation of church fellowship, " Through Him we both have access by one Spirit unto the Father," is not thought a sufficient bond of union. In other words, a heartfelt belief that there is One Being *from* whom all blessings proceed—one Mediator *in* whom all blessings are contained, and through whom they come—one Spirit *by* whom alone they can be communicated to the church and all its members, has been considered too lax a test; and outward acts, which may be shared in equally by the hardened and by the penitent, have been substituted in its place. The idea is nevertheless rapidly gaining ground that unity of spiritual basis may co-exist with disunity of church superstructure; and that sectarianism, or different outward development, is clearly distinguishable from that spirit of faction and theological rancour which is hateful in the sight of God.

So long, however, as the notion is permitted, that any bodily forms or external conformities can either make or maintain a Christian, there can be no lasting union between sects. Men may in theory regard these as secondary things only, but in practice they will ever be held as rallying points of main interest. We can become Christians only by inward faith, and not by compliance with any ceremonial acts, outward tests, or church creeds, in which the flesh may unite, whilst the soul is unquickened. If really subject unto Christ—unto Him who is "the head over all things unto the church, which is his body" (Eph. i. 22), the living branches and living members will be everywhere known by their faith and by their fruits; and by these, and not by external performances, will the church visible on earth be recognized.

Communion with God, in the largest and fullest sense of that word, (says Professor Maurice)\* is not an instrument of attaining some higher end, but is itself the end to which He is leading his creatures, and after which his creatures in all kingdoms, nations, and languages, by all their schemes of religion, by all their studies of philosophy, by art, by science, by watching, by weeping, by struggling and by submitting, by wisdom and by folly, in the camp and in the closet, in poverty and in riches, in honour and in shame, in health and in sickness,—are secretly longing and crying, and without which they cannot be satisfied."

That this communion with God has been known and felt by men in every Christian sect is an incontrovertible fact; and *because* it has been so felt, the believers in each section have longed to bring others into their fold, that they may enjoy the same blessed experience. This justifies not only the extreme love we bear to that particular religious community wherein we ourselves have realized the heavenly presence, but our anxiety to make proselytes. It is nevertheless my firm conviction, that as *communion* with God implies not only our access unto

---

\* Rev. F. D. Maurice's Seven "Letters to a Friend," &c.

God, but also the access unto us of the Holy Spirit, and as it is upon the latter that our *joy* in the Lord must depend, so the silent congregational waiting upon God is the one form in which the "communion of the Holy Ghost" (2 Cor. xiii. 14) can have the most unrestrained and undisturbed exercise.

From these remarks on what I believe to be the fundamental church-error which pervades *The Peculium*, we will turn to the work itself. Had the author perused the standard folios of Fox, Penn, and Barclay, instead of the "dumpy quartos" of enemies and seceders, he would have been preserved from many pitfalls. The strong attempt made by him in many parts of his essay to separate these three Quaker leaders is as unjustifiable chronologically, as it is religiously. P. 14 states, "One period we might call Foxite Quakerism, another Penn and Barclayite Quakerism; and p. 166—"In their *second* generation, their scholastic and apologetic period, they grounded every tenet upon the Bible," &c. The facts are simply these: Fox began to preach in 1650, and continued in full vigour until 1690, when he died. Penn joined the Friends in 1666,—they held intimate and unbroken friendship for twenty years, and nine tenths of Penn's theological writings were published in Fox's lifetime. Barclay became a Friend in 1667, and wrote his celebrated *Apology* in 1675. He died in 1690, a few months before Fox; and in 1677 these three men travelled together on the continent, preaching and spreading their Quaker principles, and distributing each other's writings.

The second serious error made is (pp. 49, 50), that all primitive Quakers believed "that every man or woman who consciously submits to the light of the Lord in their spirits, must, by the irresistible power of that Lord, be

drawn into communion and fellowship with Quakers."\*
P. 131 :—" George Fox and his fellows handed over to
the devil the whole of Christ's kingdom between the
death of the apostles and the reformation."† P. 175
speaks of " their implicit damnation of all the christened
and unchristened ;" and p. 172, that " they claimed
to be the one Holy Church, the only ark of salvation ;"‡
and that modern Quakers " would be liars and deceivers
if they were again to proclaim their Society to be the
ark of salvation, the only church of God."

In refutation of these tremendous accusations, I reply,
firstly, that if any *primitive* Quaker ever asserted his
Society to be the only ark of salvation, he was unquestionably a "liar and deceiver" against the first principle
of Fox, Penn and Barclay. These all denied that under
the gospel there was *any* outward "ark of salvation" at
all. They had no form of admission into church fellowship, and did not even call themselves a distinct church,

---

\* The following quotations disprove all of these charges :—

"*All* that believe in the light of Christ as he commands are in the election, and sit under the teaching of the grace of God which brings their salvation" (Fox's Journal, folio ed., p. 218). "These are members of the true church who know the work of regeneration in the operation and feeling of it. But they that live in the state that Adam was in the fall come not to the church which is in God ; but are enemies to the cross of Christ, which is the power of God" (Ibid, p. 253).

† There may be members, therefore, of this catholic church among *all the several sorts of Christians.* . . . " Now the church in this respect hath been in being *in all generations;* for God never wanted such wit- nesses for him." . . . "The outward profession is necessary to be a member of a particular gathered church, but not to the being a member of the one catholic church" (*Barclay's Apology*, prop. x).

‡ Neither is every visible society making profession of religion, nor all of them together, the church ; but such alone who are washed in the blood of the Lamb, and ingrafted into the true Vine, bringing forth the fruits of holiness to the glory of Christ the Head" (Penn's works, folio ed., vol. ii., p. 268).

but a *society*. Their assertion of the universality of divine grace, through which even heathens and Turks *might* be saved, was a doctrine for which they were abused without measure.

The third charge is, "That the early Friends always spoke of Quakerism as an infallible body" (p. 41). This is an assumption of Rome, but not of the Friends. The latter believe that the Holy Spirit dwells in every section of the true church of Christ. They know, also, that He is an infallible guide ; but they deny the sophistical inference of Roman Catholicism, that *therefore* the church is infallible. It must first be proved that the church is *always* guided by Him, and by Him alone. The apostles Paul, Peter and James, were fallible as men (*vide* p. 4 in present volume), and the churches they established were fallible also ; and I can find no assertions from Fox or his fellows maintaining that either they or their Society were not liable to sin or error.

His fourth assertion, "That a Quaker must not kneel down to pray with persons of another sect" (p. 114), is contradicted by the author himself (p. 186) ; where he states that, " in their second generation, their scholastic and apologetic period (Barclay and Penn, see p. 152), they grounded every tenet of Quakerism upon the Bible, upon the testimony of the Catholic fathers, and of the liturgy of the English church. This was a virtual confession that . . . every faithful user of the national prayer-book might have the inspiration and leading of the Spirit, and yet not be led into the Quaker communion." To these words of T. Hancock I will only add, that a Friend can unite with the living prayers of members of any Christian sect.

Fifthly, It is declared (p. 161), "that nearly all enthusiasts believe (and therefore Quakers as enthusiasts) the exercise of divine powers and of divinely-ordered signs is the one ever necessary witness of the divine Spirit; (p. 186) that they were to cast out devils, work miracles, and administer divine judgments."

In refutation of this very illogical deduction,* I refer to the quotation from R. Barclay at page 10 of this essay, and would remark that modern or post-apostolic miracles are contrary to the genius of Quakerism, because they lead to the worship of the visible and the material, whilst all the miracles of Scripture point to Christ and to the invisible.

6thly. It is maintained (p. 162), "That the old Quakers had a loose and uncertain view of the Incarnation, and feared being copiers of the Man Christ Jesus;" and (p. 220) "they could hardly bring themselves to believe that the Word was made flesh."

This assertion would, if true, be so deplorable, that I would earnestly ask the reader to turn to page 8 of the present volume, and see how far the quotations there made from Penn, Barclay and Fox (which might be increased *ad libitum*), and Fox's declaration of faith at p. 11, repudiate such a charge.

If space allowed, many more quotations of a like nature might be made from *The Peculium;* but sufficient has been done to show the great caution with which this essay, to which the prize was awarded, should be read by those who seek information on the Quaker creed. It is pleasant to contrast with these the somewhat antagonistic passages wherein the writer states, " No one

---

* The sophistry which lurks in parenthetic sentences is often dangerous to a casual reader. *e. g.* The logical form of this sentence is :—1st, *Some* Quakers are enthusiasts. 2nd, *Most* enthusiasts believe divine signs, &c., necessary. 3rd, Therefore *all* Quakers must do so ! This is not the only instance of the kind in *The Peculium.*

with only an hour's acquaintance with the lives and books of the Quakers, could honestly doubt that the true *fruits* of the Divine Spirit are to be found in Quakerism (p. 11); or again, " I have no doubt that their firm faith in Christ, the light and inspirer of every human being, was the *chief* cause of their wonderful successes" (p. 155).

We will now turn to the main causes adduced by T. Hancock, as leading to the inevitable extinction of Quakerism:—

1st. " If it be only a part of the Catholic church, it *is likely* to decay" (p. 8);—" Parts must die for the whole to live (p. 4). This assumption might apply to every other Christian community; but may we not prefer the old axiom, " that the whole is composed of parts," and therefore, that the vitality of the parts must add life to the whole? So long as they *are* parts or branches in union with Christ the root, they will live, even though bent and distorted by man's hands; but when disunited from Him, they wither and die.

2nd. The "prohibition of music, dancing, and theatre-going" (pp. 114, 66, &c.). Our author states that " some of the early Quakers\* pronounced all music unlawful; therefore Quakerism cannot be the *universal* kingdom for men, for it must exclude *musical men* (p. 66); in these things " the discipline of Quakerism fights against God by its prohibitions" (p. 120).

In reply to these arguments, the " discipline" does not say that sounds, sights, or movements of any kind, are sinful, *per se;* but it does assert that all three may

---

\* The sophism of converting *some* Quakers into *all* Quakers, is again apparent. In no recognized writings of the Friends is it asserted that music is " unlawful" or sinful; but it was condemned by them in the seventeenth century, as inexpedient, and injurious in practice.

be made pernicious by human contrivances. Fox and his friends well knew that under the gospel "there is nothing unclean of itself" (Rom. xiv. 14); and that to the pure all things might be pure; but they felt also, with the apostle, that although it was the gift of God, yet "if meat make my brother to offend, I will eat no flesh while the world standeth" (1 Cor. viii. 13). Very many of the grosser sins of the seventeenth century were connected with music, dancing, and theatricals; and the irreligion and immorality to which they led in the English Cavalier Court afforded ample justification for their exclusion in that day. The early Friends not only abstained from these open temptations to vice, but exhorted their members to keep from everything else which, in practice, did not conduce to the health of their souls. The lapse of two centuries has produced a change as regards music; its exclusion from amongst the Friends is no longer needful, although its undue cultivation is still very wisely discouraged.

T. Hancock states (p. 120) that the real Catholic church, so far from entirely condemning the theatre, says, "*I accept it, christen it, use it.*" That the Romish church has "used it," in the miracle plays and ecclesiastical festivals,* is most true; but there are very few Protestants who would attempt to justify scenes so

---

* The "miracle plays" were instituted in the thirteenth century, and dramatized (often in the grossest language and acting) the Annunciation— the Birth of Christ—the Crucifixion, Resurrection, and Ascension—the creation of Adam and Eve, and other sacred mysteries—and irreligious men personated the Father, the Son, and the Holy Ghost. Nothing seems to have been too holy for a stage performance; and the effects of such blasphemous representations on the minds of those who acted them needs no description.—(*See Dr. Burney's History of Music*, vol. iii), *and Hone's Ancient Mysteries Described.*) These plays still exist in some parts of Germany.—(*See A. M. Howitt's Art Student in Munich*, vol. i.)

irreverent and revolting. It is also implied (p. 66) that this Catholic church can "bless and sanctify the concert-room." I believe that no outward church can "bless or sanctify" anything—it is the prerogative of Christ alone to do this; and *if* none went to a concert, theatre, or dancing party, but those who feel that Christ does bless and sanctify it for them, such places would be unobjectionable.

3rd. That the belief of modern Quakers is entirely different from that of George Fox; and that "they have scarcely anything in common but their name and their clothes" (p. 7).

Whether this remark is as true as it is sarcastic, I will leave the reader of these pages to judge for himself. The attempt to separate the two appears to me as unfounded as the division of Fox from Barclay has been proved to be. T. Hancock assumes that to the question (p. 184), "Whether the Scriptures, *or* the Eternal Spirit who gave forth the Scriptures, would bring men to their gate?" two opposite replies would be given by the ancient and modern Friends. This assumption is incorrect; the writings of Fox, Penn and Barclay, as well as those of Gurney, Allen, and Elizabeth Fry, give one united response, viz., that *both* would.

4th, he asserts that the "tendency of the age is toward an universal society, and that the only possible religious developments of this tendency are communist societies, the Evangelical Alliance, and the Catholic church (p. 206); and that the vital question therefore is, "Can Quakers translate this tendency to Catholicity into Quakerism?" (p. 206)—"Can Quakerism preserve itself from verdict of 'Death by the tendency to Catholicity?'"

If the idea of the one church of Christ shadowed forth

in this supplemental chapter be a correct one, the Friends may give an emphatic *Yes* to both of these queries. Many branches, but one Root—many systems, but one centre, has been the characteristic of the churches of Jerusalem, Rome and Alexandria—of the seven churches in Asia,—of the Waldenses, and other churches of the dark ages—and of the different Protestant churches or sects in the present day. The Quaker church upholds this theory more clearly than any existing sect, and though opposed to communist societies—though absolutely shut out from the Evangelical Alliance, and though entreated by Churchmen to return to the Anglo-Catholic church, which professes the same fundamentals—yet, if true to itself, and to its scripture doctrine of spiritual regeneration and spiritual baptism, as the only evidence of fellowship with Christ and with his church on earth, Quakerism must yet exert an influence on the age, mightier than that of the seventeenth century, and its creed will become the centre of that catholicity towards which the age is tending.

It is also maintained by the author of *The Peculium* that "the tendency of the age is towards ritualism," and that it is also æsthetic: that "Quakerism is pledged to an incessant war against both;—and that in this war Quakerism must lose" (p. 225). To this I might add (in a similar form) that the "tendency of the age" is grasping, is warlike, is money-getting; and that Quakerism is, or ought to be, opposed to all of these. So far as an æsthetic life is consistent with a *primary* devotedness unto God, the principles of Friends admit it; but it is the duty of every church to resist, and not to yield to, the shoutings of the age towards ritualism, war, or any other thing contrary to the New Testament. All those tendencies which are in accordance with the teachings of Christ, the Friends are bound to advance; but all that are opposed to it they are bound resolutely to withstand.

There are two other subjects not specially alluded to in *The Peculium*, but which have been strongly insisted upon by other essayists; viz., the exclusion of church music, and the want of a paid ministry.

1st, *On Church Music and Singing.*—In favour of the almost universal practice of singing, it is urged that it has an uniting effect upon a congregation—that its harmonizing influence prepares the soul for worship—that it is something in which all may join, and that it was ordained of God as an integral part of divine worship amongst the Jews.

The fact of its having formed part of the worship in the old temple renders its fitness very questionable now. The Jewish temple itself is declared to be typical of the living church of Christ—of that spiritual house composed of lively stones (1 Pet. ii. 5), of which the Apostle Paul declares, " Know ye not that ye are the temple of God, and that the Spirit of God dwelleth in you? If any man defile the temple of God, him shall God destroy; for the temple of God is holy, *which temple ye are* (1 Cor. iii. 16, 17). The church in the third century having ignored this, and reintroduced the sacredness of earthly buildings, very many of the ceremonies of the old temple were also thrust, in their raw and untranslated state, into Christian worship. The forms of that Jewish and typical worship wherein the times, the places and the modes, were all ordained of God, have been grafted on, and made constituent parts of, a religion which needs them not; for at all times, in all places, and without ceremonies, we may now " have access by one Spirit unto the Father." The temple itself being changed, there must of necessity be a change also in the performances;* and every type and symbol of the old law, and the old temple, with its altar, its services and burnt offerings, its priests and its singers, its sacerdotal robes, candlesticks, incense and ornaments, must each be represented by a doctrine, an antitype, and a reality, in the new economy.

I am far from denying the stimulating effects of church music in which all the congregation join; but there are great necessary difficulties connected with it. The unconverted condition of very many who are engaged to sing praises they do not feel—the appearance of a band of instrumental performers in a Christian congregation, and the employment of the musical machinery of an organ or harmonium, seems scarcely apostolic in practice; whilst the blame bestowed upon devout Christians who sing "out of tune," the praise to the irreligious who excel in song, and the circumstance of many pious believers being unable to sing at all, prove that for this mode of worshipping God a good voice is more essential than a renewed heart. It may be said that God hears

* There were 288 singers in the temple, all of the tribe of Levi, and appointed like the priests "in their courses," twelve for every hour of the day and night (1 Chron. xxv). Is not this typical of that spiritual song of praise which all church members who are washed from their sins, and made kings and priests unto God" (Rev. i. 6), should sing in the spiritual building or temple of the Holy Ghost? Songs composed of many voices and notes, and many instruments of different hearts; but all swelling into harmonious chords, either of joy or sadness, prayer or thanksgiving. Is not some such idea as this more correct as an antitype of temple singing, than that of a choir of persons assembled to chaunt anthems, which, beautiful as they may be and are, can be joined in and sung by the unregenerate and irreligious whose human voices are musical; and which often descend into sacred musical concerts, publicly advertized, in which the exquisite performance is the main attraction.

only the hearts that breathe, and not the tongues that utter song; but that the former are quickened into worship by the harmony of human voices. Whilst I doubt not that many souls unite in hymns in which they cannot vocally join, and do thus praise the Almighty through this and other human stimulants, we have clear evidence that music is not an *essential* adjunct to the worship of God through Jesus Christ. Without condemning others, the Friends consider it inexpedient to adopt this practice, and that " the worship of the Father in spirit and in truth" can be most truly performed without it.

2nd. *On a Paid Ministry.* As stated in the foregoing essay (p. 95), the Friends support their ministers when travelling on the service of the gospel; but they hold also that a regular salary for preaching is opposed to the command of Christ, and to the spirit of the gospel. The objections made to this assumption are, that a spiritual labourer is worthy of temporal stipend, and also that without such provision God's vineyard would be neglected.

On the second difficulty, I would observe, that for two centuries of their existence, the Society of Friends has had a larger proportion of ministers than any other Christian sect\*—that these have been gathered from the rich and from the poor—that they have been engaged from home for months, and even years together, in preaching the gospel of Christ.

That he who devotes time and talent for the souls of others should reap carnal things in return, seems very plausible; but it is not so if we probe the matter a little

---

\* The number of acknowledged ministers amongst the Friends is now about 240, or one out of every fifty-seven members. Besides these, there are many unrecognized as ministers who preach.

deeper. The first and insurmountable objection is, that it makes the service of Christ a matter of business, and that young men are educated and trained for it in the same way that they are brought up to earthly callings. Although no Churchman is admitted into the ministry unless he believes " he is inwardly moved by the Holy Ghost to take upon him this office and ministration," and also that " he is truly called according to the will of our Lord Jesus Christ :"\* and although a somewhat similar declaration is required of Dissenters; yet we have abundant evidence, from the confessions of ministers themselves, as well as from ocular demonstration, that the education without the call is too generally thought sufficient.†

---

\* Book of Common Prayer—Ordination of Priests and Deacons.

† The descriptive terms made use of confirm this painful truth; *e. g.*, The gospel ministry is styled a " profession ;" a cure of souls is denominated a *living ;* and the invariable question on church preferment is, " How much is it worth ?" while the occasional preaching of Christ's gospel is called *doing duty* one for another, and the care of the flock is an *incumbency,* or a " *benefice.*" The conventional laws which permit a clergyman to add to his income by taking pupils, and writing for newspapers and periodicals, or by speculations in mines, railways, and Government stocks, entirely forbid his engaging in ordinary avocations, which are less absorbing than the former, and less hurtful than the latter. Until lately, attendance at the ball-room and the theatre, fox-hunting and banquets, have been sanctioned in a minister, in whom Paul's occupation of tentmaker, or Luke's as physician, would be utterly condemned. These unapostolic ideas have also nourished the false impression, that a holy or dedicated man cannot engage in business ; and as a corollary, that business in any form is unholy, if not sinful (see *ante*) The establishment of a clerical order, to whom "open business" is forbidden, has thrown a sacerdotal character over Christian preachers, often making them as "lords over God's heritage," rather than "being amongst them as him that serveth." Business pursuits are thought too absorbing for parish oversight or for religious study; but since many of the most studious and scientific men are connected with trade, and since they often devote more time to philanthropic and secular things than is given by

Having thus glanced at the main difficulties advanced against Quakerism, I will recapitulate the work which I believe it has yet to accomplish. In order to fulfil its mission, it is of extreme importance that an equal value should no longer be placed upon those inward principles which are unchangeable, and upon outward practices which will vary from age to age. The more the Society binds itself to principles, and the less it binds itself to practices; the more it grows from the centre outwards, and the less it tries to build from the circumference inwards; the greater must its expansive strength become. The three primary truths for which it has specially to contend are—

> 1st. That the indwelling of the Holy Spirit in the Church and in the believer is the source of all spiritual vitality.

most ministers to theology or district visiting, it is evident that all that is needful is to turn their superfluous time and talents to the service of Christ, and to allow them to labour in the inner as well as the outer courts. The advantages attendant on a paid ministry have been greatly over-estimated. Pluralities of livings, and the chance of rich benefices, have brought many carnal and irreligious men into the church who have done injury to the cause of Christ. But with hundreds of the most pious and devoted men the pay is not the temptation. Many would become ministers without it, because "the love of Christ constraineth them;" and they labour on, zealously and unheeded, and without hope of worldly preferment. If the usages of society did not interfere with the laws of Providence, and prevent their engaging in any business avocation, many of these brave-hearted men, whose families now live in penury, would, by the blessing of God on their temporal concerns, be living in comfortable independence. Satisfied am I that every preacher who is "truly called according to the will of our Lord Jesus Christ," will be provided for in temporal things; and that, if human laws and notions did not obstruct, it would be experienced by the ministers of all other denominations as it has been for two centuries by those of the Friends—"Seek ye the kingdom of God, and all these things shall be added unto you" (Luke xii. 31).

2nd. That every type of the old dispensation of Mount Sinai represents a *doctrine* (not another type) under the new dispensation of Mount Calvary.

3rd. That no intermediate helps, either of men, places, or things, are requisite for divine worship, under the gospel. That each individual soul may draw nigh unto the Father, through Christ, and needs no intervening mediums; for the Spirit itself helpeth our infirmities, and maketh intercession for us (see Rom. viii.); and that in silent worship would every Christian sect most fully realize the words of John :—" Truly our fellowship is with the Father and with his Son Jesus Christ" (1 John i. 3).

The first of these truths must be unflinchingly upheld by the Friends, but it need no longer be the battleground of Quakerism. Churchmen of every grade, and Dissenters of nearly every class, acknowledge its importance; and united prayers for the outpouring of the Holy Spirit on congregations and on individuals, are now daily offered throughout the whole kingdom.

The second thesis is probably of more importance now than it ever was, and, the whole energies of Quakerism must be put forth in its support. " The tendency of the age is ritual and æsthetic;" fascinating emblems and symbols are placed before us as representations of unseen realities, which, as in past ages, will lead to substituting the visible shell for the invisible kernel. The insufficiency and non-necessity\* of an out-

---

\* As already observed, water baptism cannot be *needful* to a Christian believer, since none of the twelve disciples were so baptized of Christ; neither could the water baptism administered by them (John iv.) have been that " of the Father, Son, and Holy Ghost," because the Holy Ghost was not yet given" (John vii. 39); and the disciples did not then

ward baptism and supper must be preached by the Friends in a bolder form than ever. History abundantly proves, that, whilst Christianity demands spiritual men, forms have produced ceremonial ones. Christianity compels change of heart, sacraments compel outward conformity. They who administer, and they who receive such, have had, *ipso facto*, a halo of holiness thrown around these which truth could not sanction; and so long as them types exist, so long will unregenerate men claim for themselves, by virtue of certain mystical rites, those blessed promises applicable to him who is " born of the Spirit," and who, having eaten his flesh and drank His blood, dwelleth in Christ and Christ in him (John vi. 56). The gospel is a spiritual religion; and no one ever partook of these rites, *spiritually*, without becoming a member of Christ's body; but throughout every age, men have partaken of them outwardly, and yet remained reprobates.

Of the third proposition the Friends must also continue the firm and unwavering defenders. It strikes at the root of all ecclesiastical intolerance and hierarchical pretensions; it denies that saints, sacred buildings, or holy things, have any virtue in conveying prayer onwards to heaven; and proclaims the doctrine that the feeblest

believe in the crucifixion or resurrection of Christ, as we are told, repeatedly, that "they understood none of these things," (Luke xviii. 39; Mark ix. 32, &c.). That the Friends unite with the apostle Paul's construction of the words, " Go and teach all nations, baptizing them," &c., is evident, since, in performing its first portion (viz., teaching all nations), he only baptized about ten of all his Corinthian converts; he also states that "though in nothing behind the very chiefest apostle," Christ sent him not to baptize. (1 Cor. i. 17). So many Jewish customs were retained by the other apostles, such as casting lots, laying on of hands, anointing with oil, purifications, circumcision, vows, &c., &c., that no Gentile law can be educed from those practices.—(See also notes pp. 19 and 20).

G

prayer, breathed by a man as he walks the busy street, may be heard on high. It also contains the blessed principle of silent worship. This latter is to be advanced, not by condemning other modes, but by inducing other religious communities to intermingle it with their own. The comfort of a few minutes' silent prayer and praise from an united congregation would be powerfully felt; and it is to this amalgamation that the attention of other sects should be invited.

To spread abroad these and other special views before alluded to, the aggregate number of the Friends may appear very small; but in reflecting on the results they accomplish in fields of philanthropy, I am brought to the conviction that if their energies are once more centred in the one object of advancing Christ's kingdom upon earth, they have ample material of every kind needful for the work. The Friends are not degenerate in principles, but in practices. If gospel truths are still committed unto them, "it is not reason that they should leave the word of God, and serve tables" (Acts vi. 2). A great deal of time and strength is now lost in discussing secondary questions, and "order and discipline" absorb the minds of very many who are formed for loftier occupation. Every member of the church has a work also to perform towards the world; and though not "all prophets, nor all teachers, neither have all the gift of tongues," it is the duty of every cleansed sinner to "go and tell how great things the Lord hath done for him." Human efforts are the ordained means for advancing the Gospel. The command, "Go ye, and teach all nations," and the prayer that the "Lord of the harvest would send forth labourers into his harvest" (Luke x. 2), prove that man is the means appointed for bringing souls unto Christ. George Fox declared that his mission was to *bring men to Christ,* and to leave them there. Human agency is thus clearly recognized. Although God miraculously struck down Paul, and appeared in a supernatural vision to Cornelius, it was yet ordained that the Gospel should be revealed to them by the lips of two fellow-men. Ananias was sent to the former, " that he might be filled with the Holy Ghost ;" and of Peter it was declared by the angel to Cornelius, " He [not I] shall tell thee what thou oughtest to do" (Acts x. 6). The besetting sin of the Friends is not that they "run without being sent ;" but that, "as good stewards of the manifold grace of God," they do not freely impart their spiritual wealth unto the hungry and the thirsty, the stranger and the naked, the sick and the imprisoned of Satan.

Far be it from me to assert that man is the *first cause* in conversion. The Spirit regenerates, but in effecting his end He avails of human agents : preachers and teachers, the learned and the ignorant, the old and the young, are all invited to take some part or other in this agency. " They that be wise shall shine as the brightness of the firmament ; and they that *turn many to righteousness,* as the stars for ever and ever." (Dan. xii. 4).

FINIS.

LONDON : A. W. BENNETT, BISHOPSGATE STREET WITHOUT.

www.ingramcontent.com/pod-product-compliance
Lightning Source LLC
Chambersburg PA
CBHW021938160426
43195CB00011B/1138